Beating the ~~What's~~
for Supper?" Blues:

A Meal Planning
Cookbook

Angie Brewster Reed

PublishAmerica
Baltimore

First printing

ISBN: 1-4137-1778-0
PUBLISHED BY PUBLISHAMERICA, LLLP
www.publishamerica.com
Baltimore

Printed in the United States of America

Dedicated to my loving family and my supportive friends at Northside Christian Church and Xenia Community Schools

Table of Contents

Author's Note

Cooking meals for your family takes planning. Although planning is not normally my thing, I do take the time to plan my family's meals. To me, it is time well spent to plan a week's worth of meals, make a grocery list, clip my coupons, and head to the store to stock my kitchen for the week. If I didn't have my meals planned, I would spend the afternoon wondering what I could make for supper and if I have what I need to make it. Trying to work while having the nagging voice of "What's for supper, Mom?" running through my brain makes me crazy. I will do just about anything to not be crazy at work since I teach 8th graders! Sometimes I let myself fall into my old habit of "flying by the seat of my pants" when it comes to meal planning—I let myself run out of groceries, don't plan my meals, don't make a list, and it **always** makes me crazy.

I've been planning my meals for about 10 years now and realized that I wanted to change the way I plan my meals and make my lists. What I actually wanted was a shortcut. I wanted to be done making my lists every week. I wanted to have a **reference** that would contain a meal plan for each week, a weekly shopping list, and the recipes I needed to make those meals. When I couldn't find what I wanted to buy, I decided to write it myself; after all, how else can I be certain that my family will like the recipes?

Sincerely,
Angie Reed

Getting Started

If you haven't ever planned meals for your family, this may seem a bit too "Martha" for you. Believe me, as much as I admire and enjoy the magazine and shows, I am **not** her. I am not an early riser, I don't have an immaculate house, I only grow easy stuff in my garden, I don't have everything organized into clear, labeled storage boxes, and I can't sew. Pretty much, the only things I plan are my teaching units and my meals. I don't even pick out my clothes the night before. If I can do this, so can you!

The first thing you need to do is make sure you have food in the house. I know that sounds pretty obvious, but we have to begin at the beginning. You need to stock up on "the basics." There are three main areas of your kitchen where your basics will be stored. These areas are the refrigerator, the spice/seasonings cabinet, and the pantry. Your pantry doesn't have to be a separate room; it can be a closet with shelves, or your cabinets. I have cabinets, but always refer to the things I store in them as my "pantry items." How you store them is up to you; I don't have a plan for that! Take the lists of basics for each area and compare them to what you already have. Write down what you need on an index card or in a composition book. Check your coupons and go shopping!

For the weekly shopping lists, I will assume that you have these basics and won't include them in the list of what you need to buy to cook your meals. Although you will probably have enough of the basics to come up with breakfasts and you will have leftovers to eat for lunch, my lists only include what you need to make your family's evening meals; not snack, breakfast or lunch items.

You may notice that I go easy on the sugar and white flour and don't include a dessert with the meals. I try to limit those things for myself because I feel better when I do. This book is not intended to be a diet or weight loss program or endorse an existing diet or weight loss plan. There is a dessert section at the end with recipes for those times when you want one to make or to take somewhere. I have not been successful in getting my family to eat fish, so you won't find any fish recipes here. Feel free to insert your family's favorites wherever you see something that doesn't appeal to you. Also, I prefer to make my own side dishes and avoid the "boxed stuff," prepared deli salads, and most of the frozen section at the store; if you want to substitute these items when the menu plan calls for coleslaw, scalloped potatoes, French fries or any other side dish that can be replaced with a convenience item—go for it! Just remember to amend the shopping list and paper clip your recipe to the recipe section (or keep it where you can find it!).

I have organized this reference into 13 weekly menu plans with the shopping lists and recipes following. Although there are 13 weeks planned, there are not 91 different meals. Some meals are repeated since they are often requested, convenient, or economical.

I don't use any fancy equipment in my kitchen, but I do rely on the following list of appliances and will assume that you have them.

Bread machine	Crock pot
Hand mixer	Blender
Mini food processor	Microwave
Free-standing mixer	Electric knife

THE REFRIGERATOR

Milk	Celery
Butter	Carrots
Eggs	Soy sauce
Yellow mustard	Worcestershire sauce
Dijon mustard	Lemon juice
Ketchup	Grated Parmesan cheese
Italian salad dressing	Cottage cheese

Ranch salad dressing   Mozzarella cheese
Cream cheese   Cheddar cheese
Barbeque sauce   Salsa
Wheat flour tortillas   Bacon
Sour cream   Pickles
Whipped salad dressing like Miracle Whip
(or mayonnaise if you prefer it)

These three items should not be kept in the refrigerator, but I'm putting them here because they are fresh vegetables and you will be able to get them when you get your carrots and celery in the produce section of your grocery store.

Potatoes   Garlic cloves
Onions

THE SPICE/ SEASONINGS CABINET

Basil	Allspice	Oregano
Paprika	Salt	Ginger
Pepper	Garlic powder	Chili powder
Cumin	Bay leaves	Dill
Cinnamon	Cilantro	Seasoning salt
Rosemary	Accent	Sesame seeds
Lemon pepper	Thyme	Dry mustard
Vanilla	Crushed red pepper flakes	

Angie's spice rub (see appendix)   Dry onion soup mix
Dry ranch dressing mix   Taco seasoning mix
Dry Italian salad dressing

Pantry Items

Cornstarch
Baking soda
Sugar
Olive oil
Flour
Dry milk
Balsamic vinegar
White vinegar
Baking mix
Taco shells
Brown rice
Oats
Bread crumbs
Crushed tomatoes
Spaghetti noodles
Corn bread mix
Chicken broth
Croutons

Baking powder
Yeast
Brown sugar
Canola oil
Confectioner's sugar
Red wine vinegar
Cider vinegar
Cooking sherry
Crackers
Peanut butter
Wild rice
Diced tomatoes
Tomato sauce
Green beans
Green chilies
Tomato soup
Beef broth

Diced tomatoes with green chiles
Cream of mushroom soup   Cream of chicken soup
Crisco sticks (butter or regular)
Whole wheat or wheat blend flour
Bread machine flour
Macaroni & cheese boxed dinner

Week 1

1. Roast pork with sauerkraut
    a. Mashed potatoes
    b. Green beans

2. Crustless spinach quiche
    a. Herb roasted potatoes

3. Cincinnati chili over hot dogs
    a. Oven fries
    b. Veggies and dip

4. Chili with spiral pasta (use leftover Cincinnati chili)
    a. Tossed salad

5. Baked chicken breasts
    a. Frozen broccoli with butter sauce
    b. Brown and wild rice

6. Taco pizza
    a. Tortilla chips and salsa

7. Oriental Hamburger
    a. Crunchy salad with garbanzos

Shopping List for Week 1

6-8 Boneless pork loin chops
1 Granny Smith apple
10 oz. Frozen chopped spinach
16 oz. Monterey Jack cheese
1 lb. cubed fully cooked ham
10 lb. potatoes
½ lb. bulk pork sausage
15 oz. tomato sauce
16 oz. cheddar cheese
1 pkg. hot dog buns
1 head Romain Lettuce
Salad vegetables (your choice)
1 pckg. dry ranch dip mix
Wheat germ
Cornmeal
6 oz. tomato paste
1 envelope taco seasoning mix
Fresh tomato (red or yellow)
Miracle Whip salad dressing
2 lbs. small red potatoes
1 bunch green onions
3 (8 oz.) cans sliced water chestnuts
16 oz. bag chow mein noodles
2 cans (15 oz.) garbanzo beans
8 oz. pkg fresh bean sprouts
Family-sized cream of mushroom soup
16 oz. package frozen French-style green beans
2 (13½ oz.) Wheat blend spiral pasta
10 ½ oz. cream of chicken soup

1 dozen eggs
8 oz. fresh mushrooms
3 lb. bag onions
2 lbs. carrots
32 oz. jar sauerkraut
2 (16 oz.) cans green beans
1 bag tortilla chips
1 can beer (optional)
1 pkg. hot dogs
1 bunch celery
1 head iceberg lettuce
16 oz. Sour cream
Dry bread crumbs
Grated Parmesan cheese
Cream of chicken soup
Diced tomatoes
4 oz. can green olives
4 oz. can black olives
Dried onion flakes
½ lb. wild rice
16 oz. Refried beans
8 oz. slivered almonds
8 oz. Italian salad dressing
1 lb. brown rice

2 (10 ½ oz.) cans chicken broth
Salsa (store-bought or Angie's homemade see appendix)
6 boneless, skinless chicken breasts
(2) 2 lb. packages and 1 (½ lb.) package ground beef

Recipes for Week 1

Day 1

Roast pork with sauerkraut:

Ingredients: boneless pork loin chops; 1 Granny Smith apple, sliced; 1 onion, diced; 32 oz. jar sauerkraut, drained; 1 can or bottle of beer (optional); olive oil; salt and pepper to taste.

Directions: Heat oil in a heavy skillet. Brown the pork on both sides in oil, salting and peppering on each side. Spray sides of a roaster with cooking spray. Place half the sauerkraut, onions, and apple on the bottom of the roaster. Lay pork on top. Salt and pepper the pork again. Cover pork with remaining sauerkraut, onions and apple. If desired, pour beer over all. Cover with a lid or foil. Bake for 3-4 hours at 300 degrees.
*Note: You can make this in a crock pot and cook it on low for 8 hours.

Mashed potatoes

Ingredients: 5 lbs potatoes; salt and pepper to taste; 3/4 cup (or so) milk; 1 stick butter.

Directions: Add 2 tsp. salt to a large pot of water. Bring it to a boil. While the water is heating, wash and peel about 5 pounds of potatoes. You can leave the peel on half of them if you want more fiber and texture. Dice the potatoes and put them in the boiling water. Boil until fork-tender (20-30 minutes). Drain potatoes in a colander.

While the potatoes are draining, place a stick of butter in the bottom of the pot you cooked it in if you are using a hand mixer or in the bottom of the bowl of your standing mixer. Mash potatoes until large lumps are gone, add milk, salt, and pepper, and then mash until smooth.

Green Beans:

Ingredients: 2 16 oz. cans green beans, drained; 1 small onion, diced; 1 Tbsp. olive oil, ½ tsp. garlic powder; ½ tsp. dried basil; salt and pepper to taste.

Directions: Heat oil in a sauté pan. Add onion and cook 2 minutes. Turn heat down to medium. Add beans and seasonings. Heat thoroughly.

Day 2

Crustless spinach quiche:

Ingredients: 1 cup chopped onion; 1 cup chopped fresh mushrooms; 1 clove garlic, smashed and finely chopped; 1 tbsp. olive oil; 1 10 oz. package frozen spinach, thawed and well drained; 1 lb. finely chopped fully cooked ham; 8 eggs; 3 cups shredded Monterey Jack cheese; ¼ tsp. pepper; 1 tsp. salt. Salsa.

Directions: In a large skillet, sauté onion, garlic, and mushrooms in oil until tender. Add spinach and ham. Cook and stir until the excess moisture is gone. Cool slightly. Beat eggs in a large bowl; add cheese and mix well. Stir in spinach mixture and salt and pepper. Spread evenly in a lasagna pan that has been coated with cooking spray. Bake at 350 degrees for 40-45 minutes or until a knife inserted near the center comes out clean. Serve with salsa if desired.

Herb roasted potatoes:

Ingredients: ½ cup whipped salad dressing; 1 Tbsp. *each* dried rosemary, garlic powder, and onion flakes; 1 tsp. seasoned salt; 1 Tbsp. water; 2 lbs. unpeeled small red potatoes, washed and quartered.

Directions: Mix dressing, seasonings, and water in a large bowl. Add potatoes; toss to coat. Place potatoes on a large jellyroll pan that has been coated with cooking spray. Spray more cooking spray over the potatoes. Bake at 350 degrees for 45 minutes to an hour, stirring after 20 minutes.
*Note: If your family doesn't like rosemary, substitute dried oregano or basil.

Day 3

Cincinnati chili over hot dogs:

Ingredients: 2 lbs. ground beef; 2 onions, chopped; 1 tsp. allspice, 1 tsp. cinnamon; 1 tsp. garlic powder; 1 tsp. cayenne or red pepper flakes; 2-3 Tbsp. chili powder; 1 tsp. ground cumin; 1 Tbsp. red wine vinegar; 4 bay leaves; 1 tsp. salt; 1 tsp. pepper; 15 oz. tomato sauce; 15 oz. can diced tomatoes with green chilies; 2 cups water; hot dogs, shredded cheddar cheese; extra chopped onion; hot dog buns.

Directions: Brown ground beef and onion together; drain and transfer to a large pot. Add remaining ingredients. Bring to a boil. Reduce heat and simmer for 3 hours. Remove bay leaves. Serve over grilled hot dogs on buns. Top with shredded cheese and extra chopped onion.
*Note: I usually put this together in my crock pot the night before and cook it on low while I'm at work the next day.

Oven fries:

Ingredients: 2 lbs. potatoes, washed and cut into wedges; 1 Tbsp. seasoning salt; 2 tsp. chili powder; cooking spray.

Directions: Spray a jellyroll pan with cooking spray. Place potato wedges on pan and spray generously with cooking spray. Stir to coat with oil. Sprinkle seasonings over potato wedges. Stir to coat with seasonings; add more if necessary. Bake at 400 degrees for 45 minutes or until crispy, stirring after the first 20 minutes.

Veggies and dip

Ingredients: Carrots; celery; cucumber; 1 pint sour cream; 1 packet dry ranch dressing mix.

Directions: Peel and wash veggies. Cut carrots and celery into sticks. Slice cucumber. Mix sour cream and dry ranch dressing mix together with a fork.

Day 4

Cincinnati chili with spiral pasta:

Ingredients: Leftover Cincinnati chili; 2 13 ½ oz. boxes spiral pasta; shredded cheddar cheese; diced onion.

Directions: Reheat Cincinnati chili. Cook pasta according to the directions on the box; drain. Top individual servings of pasta with chili, onions, and cheese.

Tossed salad:

Ingredients: Romaine lettuce, carrots, cucumbers, broccoli, celery, green onion, grape tomatoes; salad dressing.

Directions: If you have leftover veggies from last night, dice them first and place them in a large bowl. Wash lettuce and dry with paper towels; tear into bite-sized pieces and add to bowl. Peel and wash other veggies; chop into bite-sized pieces (you won't need to chop the tomatoes) and add to bowl. Toss thoroughly and top with your favorite salad dressing.

Day 5

Baked chicken breasts:

Ingredients: 6 boneless, skinless chicken breasts, washed and patted dry with paper towels; 1 ¼ cups dry bread crumbs; ½ cup Parmesan cheese; 2 Tbsp. wheat germ, 2 tsp. dried basil; 1 tsp. garlic powder; 2 eggs; ¼ cup water.

Directions: Spray a shallow baking pan with cooking spray. In a pie plate, beat eggs with water. In another pie plate, mix dry ingredients. Using one hand (you always want to keep one clean), dip chicken breasts in egg and then dry ingredients, turning to coat. Place chicken in the baking pan. When all of the chicken is in the pan, spray again with cooking spray. Cook at 350 degrees for 45 minutes or until done, turning after 20 minutes.

Brown and wild rice:

Ingredients: ½ cup wild rice; 2 cups brown rice; chicken broth; 2 tsp. parsley flakes, ½ tsp. garlic powder; salt and pepper to taste.

Directions: You'll have to cook these separately and then mix them together at the end because the wild rice takes longer to cook than the brown rice. Cook each type according to its package directions, substituting chicken broth for ½ or all of the water suggested. Add the seasonings to the brown rice. When the wild rice is nearly done, add it to the brown rice and continue cooking until the rest of the liquid is absorbed. Fluff with a fork and serve.

Heat frozen broccoli with butter sauce according to package directions; salt and pepper to taste.

Day 6

Taco pizza:

Ingredients: 1 ¼ cups cornmeal; 1 ¼ cups all-purpose flour; 2 tsp. baking powder; 1 ½ tsp. salt; ⅔ cup milk; ⅓ cup butter, melted; ½ lb. ground beef; ½ lb. bulk pork sausage; 1 can (6 oz.) tomato paste; 1 can (14 ½ oz.) diced tomatoes with chiles, undrained; 1 envelope taco seasoning mix; ¾ cup water; 1 can (16 oz.) refried beans; 1 ½ cups (6 oz.) shredded cheddar cheese; 1 cup (4 oz.) shredded Monterey Jack cheese; 2 cups chopped lettuce; 1 cup diced fresh tomato (a yellow tomato is nice with this dish); ½ cup sliced black olives; ½ cup sliced green onions.

Directions: In a medium bowl, combine the cornmeal, flour, baking powder, and salt. Add the milk and butter; mix well. Press onto the bottom of a 12-14 inch pizza pan. Bake at 400 degrees for 10 minutes or until edges are lightly browned. Cool. In a large skillet, brown beef and sausage; drain. Stir in the tomato paste, canned tomatoes, taco seasoning, and water; bring to a boil. Simmer, uncovered, for 5 minutes. Heat refried beans with a little bit of the liquid from the meat mixture (you can do this in the microwave). Mash beans with a fork until they are a spreadable consistency. Spread beans over the crust. Spread meat mixture over the beans. Combine cheeses; sprinkle 2 cups over the meat layer. Bake at 400 degrees for 15 minutes or until the cheese melts. Top with lettuce, fresh tomato, olives, onions, and remaining cheese.

Serve with tortilla chips and salsa.

Day 7

Oriental hamburger:

Ingredients: 2 lbs. ground beef; 2 medium onions; 1 cup chopped celery; 1 can (10 ½ oz.) cream of chicken soup; 1 can (family-sized) cream of mushroom soup; 1 cup water; 1 cup cooked brown rice; 1 tbsp. soy sauce; 1 tsp. pepper; 1 can sliced water chestnuts; chow mien noodles.

Directions: In a large skillet, brown ground beef and vegetables; drain. Place beef mixture in a large casserole dish. Add remaining ingredients to casserole and stir until blended together. Cover and microwave at med-high heat for 20 minutes. Stir and cook 5 minutes longer. Top individual servings with chow mien noodles.

Crunchy salad with garbanzos:

Ingredients: 1 lb. carrots, julienned; 1 (16 oz.) package French-style green beans, thawed; 2 cans (15 oz. each) garbanzo beans, rinsed and drained; 1 packager fresh bean sprouts; 1 cup slivered almonds, toasted; 1 cup Italian salad dressing.

Directions: In a bowl, combine the first 5 ingredients; mix well. Add the almonds and the salad dressing, toss to coat. Cover and refrigerate until serving.

Week 2

8. Homemade pizza
    a. Veggies and dip

9. Spicy chicken
    a. Grandma Sandy's macaroni and cheese
    b. Baked beans

10. Spicy chicken salad
    a. Parmesan Focaccia

11. Hamburgers
    a. Three bean salad

12. Minestrone soup
    a. Deluxe grilled cheese

13. Stuffed bell peppers
    a. Mashed potatoes
    b. Succotash

14. Baked ham
    a. Baked sweet potatoes
    b. Pineapple casserole

Shopping List for Week 2

8 oz. pkg. turkey or reg. pepperoni
8 oz. fresh mushrooms
1 bunch broccoli
3 lbs. onions
2 cans kidney beans
2 cans green beans
10 lbs. potatoes
1 pkg. wheat hamburger buns
2 heads lettuce
Salad vegetables (your choice)
1 jar banana pepper rings
1 (10 oz.) pkg. frozen corn
1 (10 oz.) pkg. frozen Lima beans
1 quart tomato juice
6 oz. tomato paste
2 (16 oz.) cans crushed pineapple
4 oz. can sliced black olives
4 oz. can sliced green olives
1 small green cabbage
1 (10 oz.) pkg. frozen spinach
5 (10½ oz.) cans chicken broth
3-4 lb. boneless baked ham
4 boxes macaroni and cheese
16 oz. spaghetti noodles
2 (1 ½ lbs.) packages ground beef

4 prepared pizza crusts
16 oz. cheddar cheese
1 head cauliflower
2 lbs. carrots
1 can garbanzo beans
Dry ranch dressing mix
6 bell peppers
1 lb. brown rice
16 oz. sour cream
6 sweet potatoes
Dry onion soup mix
1 Red onion
6 sweet potatoes
16 American cheese slices
1 med. zucchini
Saltine crackers
Wheat Bread flour
BBQ sauce
28 oz. can diced tomatoes
1 bunch celery
16 American cheese slices
1 med. cucumber
1 lb. bacon
Ranch salad dressing
16 oz. mozzarella cheese

10 -12 Boneless, skinless chicken breasts
2 large cans of baked beans (we like Van deCamp's)
1 jar pizza sauce (we like Contadina)
1 can (16 oz.) Italian flat green beans
Butter flavored crackers (like Ritz)

Recipes for Week 2

Day 1

Homemade pizza:

Ingredients: 4 prepared pizza crusts; 1 can pizza sauce; 8 oz. turkey pepperoni; sliced onion, 16 oz. mozzarella cheese (shredded); garlic powder; fresh mushrooms; 1 sm. jar sliced black olives; 1 sm. jar sliced green olives; banana peppers.

Directions: Heat oven to 375 degrees. Spray pizza crusts with oil. Bake (2 at a time) for 5 minutes. Spread each pizza crust with ¼ of pizza sauce. Sprinkle with garlic powder. Top each pizza with 1 cup cheese, ¼ of the pepperoni, mushrooms, onions, and your desired amount of drained olives and banana peppers. Bake for 10-15 minutes. (2 at a time)

Veggies and dip

Ingredients: Carrots; celery; cucumber; broccoli, cauliflower; 1 pint sour cream; 1 packet dry ranch dressing mix.

Directions: Peel and wash veggies. Cut carrots and celery into sticks. Slice cucumber. Chop broccoli and cauliflower into florets. Mix sour cream and dry ranch dressing mix together with a fork.

Day 2

Spicy Chicken:

Ingredients: Angie's spice rub; 10-12 boneless chicken breasts.

Directions: Trim visible fat from chicken; rinse and pat dry. Place 3 chicken breasts in a large plastic container with a lid. Sprinkle with 1 Tbsp. spice rub. Cover container with lid and shake to coat chicken. Place chicken in a large foil roasting/grilling bag. Repeat until all chicken is seasoned. Bake at 450 degrees for 45 minutes. Let stand in foil 10 minutes before opening foil.
*Note: You can make this chicken on the grill (5-7 minutes per side) and then cover it in foil for 10 minutes or bake it on a sided cookie sheet covered with foil. Letting it sit for 10 minutes in the foil seems to bring out the juices. Also, you can adjust the amount of seasoning to your family's tastes. If you really want it hot, marinate the chicken in the spices for an hour or more before cooking.

Grandma Sandy's macaroni and cheese:

Ingredients: 16 oz. box spaghetti noodles, cooked according to package directions and drained; the cheese powder from 4 boxes macaroni and cheese (save the elbows for another use); 1 sleeve saltine crackers, crushed; 2 sticks butter; milk (about a quart); salt and pepper.

Directions: Spray a large glass casserole (including the underside of the lid) liberally with cooking oil. Put a layer of spaghetti noodles in the bottom of the dish, sprinkle with salt, pepper, and powdered cheese, cracker crumbs, more cheese, and dot with butter. Repeat layers, ending up with a layer of cheese on top. Pour milk over all. Take a butter knife and poke it through the layers and wiggle it. Do this all over the casserole to distribute the milk. You may need to add more milk. Cover and bake at 300 degrees for 2 ½ - 3 hours. The top and sides will be browned, but not burned.

Baked beans:

Ingredients: 2 large cans baked beans, ½ cup brown sugar; ¼ cup ketchup; ¼ cup BBQ sauce; 2 Tbsp. cider vinegar; 2 tsp. ground mustard; 1 tsp. pepper; 3 or 4 strips of bacon.

Directions: Pour excess liquid off beans and remove any chunks of pork fat. In a large bowl, mix all ingredients except bacon. Spray a rectangular pan with cooking oil and pour the bean mixture into it. Lay bacon across the top. Bake, uncovered at 300 degrees for about an hour.

Day 3

Spicy chicken salad:

Ingredients: 1 head lettuce; assorted chopped salad veggies (if you have any leftovers from Day 1 use those first); cold leftover spicy chicken; 1 cup shredded cheddar cheese; ½ cup chopped red onion; croutons or chow mein noodles; ranch salad dressing.

Directions: Dice leftover chicken. Chop veggies and tear lettuce. Toss in a large bowl. Place salad on individual plates and top with chicken, red onion, cheese, croutons or chow mien noodles, and ranch dressing.

Parmesan focaccia:

Ingredients: 3 cups wheat bread flour; ¾ cup plus 3 Tbsp. water at 80 degrees; 3 Tbsp. butter, softened; 2 Tbsp. nonfat dry milk powder; 3 Tbsp. sugar; 1 ½ tsp. salt; 3 cups wheat bread flour; 2 ¼ tsp. active dry yeast; 2 Tbsp. olive oil; 4 Tbsp. Parmesan cheese; 1 tsp. garlic salt.

Directions: In your bread machine pan, place the first 7 ingredients in the order suggested by your bread machine manufacturer. Select the dough setting (check dough after 5 minutes of mixing; add 1 to 2 Tbsp. flour or water if needed). When the cycle is completed, turn dough onto a lightly floured surface. Cover and let rest for 15 minutes. Knead for 1 minute. Roll into a 15 inch by 10 inch rectangle. Transfer to a greased 15x10x1 inch baking pan. Press dough up the sides a bit. Cover and let rise 20-30 minutes. With a wooden spoon or your fingertips, make indentations at 1 inch intervals. Brush dough with olive oil; sprinkle with garlic salt and Parmesan cheese. Bake at 400 degrees for 13-15 minutes or until lightly browned. Cool slightly. Cut into squares and serve warm.

Day 4

Hamburgers:

Ingredients: 1 ½ lbs. ground chuck; 1 Tbsp. steak seasoning; 2 Tbsp. ketchup; 1 Tbsp. Worcestershire sauce; wheat hamburger buns; lettuce; tomato; sliced red onion; and your favorite condiments.

Directions: In a large bowl, thoroughly mix meat, steak seasoning, ketchup, and Worcestershire sauce. Shape into patties. Either grill outside on a gas or charcoal grill or indoors on a George Foreman grill until burgers are well done. Serve on wheat hamburger buns with lettuce, tomato, onions, and condiments of your choice.

Three bean salad:

Ingredients: 1 can green beans; 1 can kidney beans; 1 can garbanzo beans; 3 green onions; ¼ cup red wine vinegar; 2 Tbsp. olive oil; 1 tsp. basil; 1 tsp. oregano; ½ tsp. salt; ½ tsp. pepper; ½ tsp garlic powder.
Directions: In a small bowl, whisk vinegar, oil, and seasonings together. Drain and rinse beans. Chop onions. Combine all together and chill for at least half an hour. Serve with a slotted spoon.

Day 5

Minestrone Soup:

Ingredients: 1 Tbsp. olive oil; 1 cup diced onion; 1 Tbsp. minced garlic (about 3 cloves); 1 cup diced carrots; 1 cup diced celery; 1 cup diced zucchini; 3 cups shredded cabbage; 2 tsp. oregano; 1 ½ Tbsp. basil; 2 tsp. salt; 1 tsp. black pepper; ½ tsp. thyme; 1 bay leaf; 7 cups chicken broth; 28 oz. can diced tomatoes; 14 ½ oz. can Italian flat beans; ½ small frozen package of spinach; 15 oz. can kidney beans; 1 ½ cups macaroni noodles (you can use the leftover noodles from the macaroni).

Directions: Heat oil in a large soup pot over medium heat. Add diced onion and garlic; sauté until soft. Add celery and carrots, cook for about 5 minutes. Add zucchini and cook for about 3 minutes. Add shredded cabbage and cook for about 5 minutes. Add seasonings, broth, and tomatoes. Lower heat and cook for 2 hours. Add drained green beans, rinsed and drained kidney beans, and spinach. Continue cooking for 20 minutes more. Cook pasta in a separate pan of boiling water for about 8 minutes. Drain and add to soup. This makes a lot of soup, but you can freeze the leftovers in freezer bags.

Deluxe grilled cheese:

Ingredients: 12 slices wheat bread; 12 slices American cheese; butter; brown sugar.

Directions: Heat a griddle or a George Foreman grill. Butter one side of each slice of bread. Place 6 slices of bread butter-side down on the griddle or grill. Top each slice with 2 slices American cheese and about 2 tsp. brown sugar. Cover brown sugar with 6 slices of bread butter-side up. Grill for about 1-2 minutes on each side.

Day 6

Stuffed bell peppers:

Ingredients: 6 bell peppers; 1 ½ lbs. ground beef; ½ cup brown rice; 1 tsp. black pepper; 1 Tbsp. Worcestershire sauce; ½ cup ketchup; 1 envelope dry onion soup mix; tomato juice.

Directions: In a large saucepan, bring 2 quarts of water to a boil. While you are waiting for the water to boil, make the rice according to the package directions. Cut the tops off the peppers and place in boiling water for about 5 minutes. Brown ground beef and drain. In a large bowl, mix beef, rice, ketchup, pepper, Worcestershire sauce, and onion soup mix. Place bell peppers in the bottom of a large covered casserole dish or roasting pan. Fill each pepper with ground beef mixture and pour tomato juice (about a quart) over all. Cover and bake at 350 degrees for 1 hour.

31

Note: you can also put this together the night before in the crock pot and let it cook on low all day.

Mashed potatoes:

Ingredients: 5 lbs potatoes; salt and pepper to taste; 3/4 cup (or so) milk; 1 stick butter.

Directions: Add 2 tsp. salt to a large pot of water. Bring it to a boil. While the water is heating, wash and peel about 5 pounds of potatoes. You can leave the peel on half of them if you want more fiber and texture. Dice the potatoes and put them in the boiling water. Boil until fork-tender (20-30 minutes). Drain potatoes in a colander. While the potatoes are draining, place a stick of butter in the bottom of the pot you cooked it in if you are using a hand mixer or in the bottom of the bowl of your standing mixer. Mash potatoes until large lumps are gone, add milk, salt, and pepper, and then mash until smooth.

Succotash

Ingredients: 1 package frozen corn; 1 package frozen lima beans; butter.

Directions: Microwave vegetables according to package directions. Mix together and top with about a tablespoon of butter.

Day 7

Baked ham:

Ingredients: 1 small boneless ham, ¼ cup brown sugar.

Directions: Rinse ham and rub with brown sugar. Place in a heavy pan and cover with foil. Bake at 350 degrees for about 2 ½ - 3 hours. Allow to stand for 15 minutes before slicing. Slice with an electric knife.

Baked sweet potatoes:

Ingredients: 6 sweet potatoes; butter; cinnamon.

Directions: Scrub and pierce potatoes. Wrap each in foil. Bake for 1 hour at 350 degrees. Top each with butter and cinnamon.

Pineapple casserole:

Ingredients: 2 (16 oz.) cans crushed pineapple; 1 cup sugar; ¾ cup flour; 1 cup grated cheddar cheese; 1 sleeve butter flavored crackers (crushed); 1 stick butter (melted).

Directions: Generously grease an oblong casserole dish. Mix all ingredients except crackers and butter in a large bowl and pour into the greased dish. Top with crackers and drizzle butter over crackers. Bake at 350 degrees for 30 minutes.

Week 3

15. Grilled smoked sausage
     a.   Grilled potatoes
     b.   Grilled pepper salad

16. Angie's black (or red) beans
     a.   Brown rice

17. Very garlicky chicken
     a.   Italian bread
     b.   Tomato and cucumber salad

18. Crock-pot meatloaf
     a.   Baked potatoes
     b.   Green bean casserole

19. Muffuletta Sandwich
     a.   Potato chips

20. Roast beef with vegetables
     a.   Beer biscuits

21. Shredded beef sandwiches (uses leftover roast)
     a.   Sweet potato fries
     b.   Cole slaw

Shopping List for Week 3

2 (1½ lb.) pkgs. beef smoked sausage
6 oz. can frozen orange juice concentrate

1 lb. dry black (or red) beans	4 sweet potatoes
1 quart can tomatoes in juice	4 garlic bulbs
Miracle Whip	3 lbs. ground beef
Old fashioned oats	1 dozen eggs
Ketchup	8 oz. mozzarella cheese
2 large cans green beans	2 lbs. carrots
1 large can cream of mushroom soup	3 lbs. onions
1 canister French fried onions	1 lb. brown rice
Grated Parmesan cheese	1 bunch celery
Your favorite potato chips	1 (10½ oz.) can beef broth
16 oz. sour cream	1 (10½ oz.) chicken broth
10 lbs. potatoes	Bisquick baking mix
1 bottle of beer	1 bunch green onions
1 envelope dry Italian dressing mix	3 fresh tomatoes
6 oz. can pitted black olives	1 med. cucumber
5 oz. jar pimento stuffed green olives	9 inch round loaf bread
Wheat sandwich buns	1 small green cabbage
1(15 oz.) can tomato sauce	Red wine vinegar
¼ lb. deli ham	¼ lb. sliced hard salami
¼ lb. sliced Provolone cheese	¼ lb. sliced Swiss cheese
2 red onions	Fresh chives

Wooden or metal skewers for grilling
8 pieces bone-in chicken (a whole chicken cut up will work)
2 envelopes dry beefy onion soup mix
4 bell peppers (2 green, 1 red, and 1 yellow)
2 (3-4 lb.) bottom or top round roasts

Recipes for Week 3

Day 1

Grilled smoked sausage:

Ingredients: 2 packages beef smoked sausage

Directions: Cook over a medium–hot grill according to package directions or until browned to your satisfaction (about 10-15 minutes at our house)

Grilled potatoes

Ingredients: 1 ½ -2 lbs potatoes; 1 bunch green onions, sliced; 1 Tbsp. olive oil; 1 large foil grilling bag; 2 Tbsp. grated Parmesan cheese; 1 tsp. oregano; 1 tsp. basil; 1 tsp. garlic salt; ½ tsp. pepper.

Directions: Scrub potatoes and cut into ½ inch cubes; place in a large bowl. Add green onions and oil; toss to coat. Combine spices and cheese; sprinkle over potatoes. Place in foil bag and seal. Cook potatoes on a medium-hot grill for 20-25 minutes or until potatoes are tender.

Grilled pepper salad

Ingredients: 1 green pepper; 1 yellow pepper; 1 red pepper; 1 red onion; 8 oz. mozzarella; 1 (6 oz.) can pitted black olives; ⅔ cup olive oil; ⅓ cup red wine vinegar; 2 Tbsp. lemon juice; 2 Tbsp. Dijon mustard; 1 tsp. basil; ½ tsp. cayenne pepper; ½ tsp. garlic powder.

Directions: Cut peppers into 1 inch pieces and thread onto metal or soaked wooden skewers; grill for 10-12 minutes or until the edges are browned. Remove from skewers and place in a salad bowl. Cut onion in half and slice thinly. Cut mozzarella into bit-sized cubes. Drain olives and cut in halves. Add onion, mozzarella, and olives; toss gently. Combine remaining ingredients in a jar with a tight-fitting lid; shake well. Pour over pepper mixture and serve.

Day 2

Angie's black (or red) beans:

Ingredients: 1 cup chopped onion; ½ cup chopped celery; ¾ cup chopped carrots; 6-8 garlic cloves, chopped; ½ cup chopped green pepper; ½ lb. smoked sausage (use leftovers from Day 1), chopped fine; 1 Tbsp. oil; 16 oz. dry black or red beans; 1 quart chopped canned tomatoes in juice; 1 tsp. salt; 1 tsp. pepper; 2-3 Tbsp. chili powder; 1 tsp. red pepper flakes; 1 tsp. cilantro; 1 tsp. paprika; 1 tsp. cumin; ½ cup frozen orange juice concentrate; 1 quart water. Serve over brown rice.
Note: this makes a lot; freeze your leftovers!

Directions: Soak beans in cold water overnight or use the quick-soak method (bring beans and water to a boil, remove from heat and let stand for 1 hour). Drain and rinse beans. Sauté veggies and sausage in oil until veggies are tender (5 minutes or so). Combine beans, veggie mixture, water, tomatoes, orange juice concentrate, and spices in a large pot. Bring to a boil. Reduce heat and simmer for 1 ½ -2 ½ hours. Serve beans over hot cooked rice.

Brown rice:

Ingredients: 3 cups brown rice; 1 tsp. salt; 6 cups water.

Directions: Combine all ingredients. Bring to a boil and simmer for about 40 minutes. Turn off heat and let stand 10 minutes. Fluff with a fork.

Day 3

Very garlicky chicken:

Ingredients: 8 pieces bone-in chicken; oil spray; 1 tsp. basil; 1 tsp salt; ½ tsp. pepper; 1 tsp. parsley; 2-3 bulbs garlic (this is the **whole head**, not cloves); 2 onions; ½ can chicken broth.

Directions: Heat oven to 375 degrees. Separate garlic bulbs into cloves and peel each clove by placing the clove on its side and mashing it down with the flat side of a large knife. Slice onions. Combine seasonings in a small bowl. Spray a baking dish and chicken with oil. Sprinkle combined seasonings on chicken. Top with garlic and onion. Pour broth on chicken (freeze the rest in a freezer bag to use another time). Cover with foil. Baked covered for 40 minutes. Uncover and bake 30 minutes more. Spread the softened garlic cloves on Italian bread.

Italian bread:

Ingredients: 1 ¼ cup water at 80 degrees; 3 Tbsp. butter, softened; 3 cups wheat bread flour; ½ cup grated Parmesan cheese; 1 Tbsp. sugar; 2 tsp. garlic salt; 1 tsp. basil; 1 tsp. oregano; 1 tsp. ground thyme; 2 ¼ tsp. yeast.

Directions: In your bread machine pan, place the ingredients in the order listed above. Choose the basic bread and light crust settings on your bread machine. Cool for about 15 minutes before slicing.

Tomato and cucumber salad:

Ingredients: 3 medium tomatoes; 1 cucumber; 1 red onion; ¼ cup olive oil; 2 Tbsp. red wine vinegar; 2 Tbsp. fresh basil or 2 tsp. dried basil; ¼ tsp. salt; ¼ tsp. pepper.

Directions: Slice tomatoes, cucumber, and onion. Layer slices in a large salad bowl. In a small bowl, whisk together oil, vinegar, and seasonings. Drizzle over veggies. Cover and refrigerate until ready to serve. Toss gently before serving.

Day 4

Crock pot meatloaf:

Ingredients: 3 lbs. ground chuck; 1 Tbsp. Worcestershire sauce; 2 envelopes dry beefy onion soup mix; 1 cup ketchup; 2 eggs; 1 cup old fashioned oats.

Directions: In a large bowl, thoroughly mix all ingredients. Shape into a loaf. Cook on low in your crock-pot for 8-10 hours. When done, remove carefully with 2 spatulas onto a serving plate.

Baked potatoes:

Ingredients: 6 large potatoes; spray cooking oil; 6 sheets foil; salt; butter; sour cream; fresh chives.

Directions: Scrub potatoes and pierce with a fork. Spray cooking oil on each sheet of foil. Sprinkle with salt. Place a potato in the center of each sheet of foil and wrap to cover potato. Bake at 375 degrees for 1 hour. Top with butter, sour cream, and fresh chives.

Green bean casserole:

Ingredients: 2 large cans green beans, drained; 1 large can cream of mushroom soup; 1 cup milk; ½ tsp. pepper; ½ tsp garlic powder; French fried onions.

Directions: In a large bowl, mix all ingredients except French fried onions. Turn into a greased casserole dish. Bake, uncovered at 375 degrees for 30 minutes. Top with French fried onions and bake 5-10 minutes more.

Day 5

Muffuletta sandwich:

Ingredients: 5 oz. jar pimiento stuffed green olives, drained and sliced; 1 tomato, seeded and chopped; 1 clove garlic, minced; 1 tsp. dried oregano; 1 tsp. dried basil; 3 Tbsp. olive oil; 2 Tbsp. Balsamic vinegar; ½ tsp. black pepper; 9 inch round loaf bread; 2 Tbsp. Miracle Whip; ¼ lb. sliced ham; ¼ lb. sliced hard salami; ¼ lb. sliced provolone cheese; ¼ lb. sliced Swiss cheese; ½ red onion, thinly sliced.

Directions: In a medium bowl, combine the first 7 ingredients; mash together with a fork until it resembles a paste. Slice the loaf of bread in half (horizontally) so you have a giant sandwich bun. Spread the inside of the top and bottom "bun" with Miracle Whip. Stack the sandwich by layering olive paste, meat, cheese and onion slices on the "bun." Wrap tightly in plastic wrap and refrigerate for 1 hour. Slice into wedges and serve with your family's favorite potato chips.

Day 6

Roast beef with vegetables:

Ingredients: 2 medium sized roasts, rinsed and excess fat removed; 6 carrots, peeled and left whole; 3 onions, peeled and cut in half; 6 potatoes, peeled and left whole; 2 envelopes dry onion soup mix; 2 Tbsp Worcestershire sauce; pepper to taste; 1 can beef broth.

Directions: Place roast beef in a large roasting pan. Sprinkle Worcestershire sauce and dry onion soup mix on all sides. Add vegetables to roasting pan and pepper to taste. Pour beef broth over all. Cover and bake at 350 degrees for 3 hours. Check every hour and add more beef broth or water as needed.
Note: you can also put this together the night before in the crock pot and let it cook on low all day.

Beer biscuits

Ingredients: 2 cups Bisquick; 2 Tbsp. sugar; 8 oz. room temperature beer.

Directions: Mix all ingredients in a medium-sized bowl. Bake biscuits in a well- greased muffin pan at 450 degrees 8-10 minutes or until done. This recipe makes a dozen biscuits, but you can double it if you need more.

Day 7

Shredded beef sandwiches:

Ingredients: Leftover roast beef from Day 6; 16 oz. tomato sauce; ½ cup ketchup; 2 Tbsp. brown sugar; 2 Tbsp. cider vinegar; 1 Tbsp. Worcestershire sauce; 1 onion, chopped fine; sandwich buns.

Directions: Place beef in a large saucepan. Shred beef with 2 forks. Add remaining ingredients and stir well. Bring to a boil and reduce heat. Simmer the beef mixture, stirring occasionally, for 2 hours or until desired consistency. Serve on sandwich buns.
Note: You can throw this in the crock pot and cook it on low for 4-5 hours.

Sweet potato fries:

Ingredients: 4 sweet potatoes; 3-4 Tbsp. olive oil; 2 tsp. salt; 2-3 tsp. chili powder.

Directions: Scrub potatoes and cut into sticks. In a large bowl, toss potato sticks with oil, salt, and chili powder. Spread potatoes on a greased baking sheet and bake at 425 degrees for 20 minutes, turning once.

Cole slaw:

Ingredients: 1 small head green cabbage; ½ a red onion; 2 carrots; ¾ cup Miracle whip; ¼ cup red wine vinegar; ½ tsp. pepper; ½ tsp. celery seed; 2 tsp. sugar.

Directions: Finely chop vegetables by hand or with a food processor; place in a large salad bowl. Mix remaining ingredients together in a medium bowl and pour over cabbage. Toss thoroughly and chill for at least 1 hour before serving.

Week 4

22. French onion soup
    a. Reuben sandwiches

23. Creamy chicken cordon bleu in a crock-pot
    a. Brown rice pilaf
    b. Peas

24. Tacos
    a. Refried bean dip and tortilla chips
    b. Fresh salsa

25. Taco salad (uses leftovers from Day 3)

26. Blueberry pancakes
    a. Bacon

27. Grilled Italian chicken breasts
    a. Herbed vegetables
    b. Garlic bread sticks

28. Chicken Alfredo (uses leftover chicken and veggies from Day 6)

Shopping List for Week 4

2 (3 lbs.) bags onions
1 ½ lbs. deli corned beef
1 Loaf rye bread
2 envelopes taco seasoning mix
32 oz. jar sauerkraut
1 (10½ oz.) can chicken broth
¼ lb. thinly sliced ham
1 lb. brown rice
6 oz. slivered almonds
2 lbs. carrots
2 lbs. cheddar cheese
Salad greens (like Romaine)
2 cucumbers
1 bunch green onions
1 can Spicy V-8 juice
Fritos chili cheese corn chips
1 head iceberg lettuce
Blueberry muffin mix
1 bunch broccoli
2 zucchini
2 (1 lb.) pkgs. fettuccini noodles
2 (4 oz.) cans diced green chiles

1 bunch celery
8 oz. Swiss cheese slices
Croutons (we like Caesar)
8 oz. mozzarella cheese
2 jars Alfredo sauce
Fresh chives
1 (10 oz.) pkg. frozen peas
1 lb. fresh mushrooms
2 lbs. ground beef
1 bag tortilla chips
Bisquick baking mix
5 tomatoes
2 jalapeno peppers
Taco shells (soft or hard)
Fresh parsley
Fresh cilantro
Catalina dressing
1 lb. bacon
Italian salad dressing
Pancake syrup
Grated Parmesan cheese
1 head cauliflower

10-12 boneless skinless chicken breasts
2 (15 oz.) cans diced tomatoes with green chilies
6 (10½ oz.) cans low sodium beef broth
1 small bottle thousand island dressing
1 family size can cream of chicken soup
2 cans refried beans (we like Rosarita)

Recipes for Week 4

Day 1

French onion soup:

Ingredients: 3 lbs. onions, skins removed, cut in half, and sliced; 2 garlic cloves, minced; 1 stick butter; 1 Tbsp. balsamic vinegar; 2 tsp. Worcestershire sauce; 1 tsp. black pepper; 6 cans beef broth (I usually use low sodium); 1 ½ cups shredded mozzarella cheese; ¼ cup grated Parmesan cheese; croutons.

Directions: Melt butter in a large pot. Add onions and garlic. Stir, cover, and cook for about 5 minutes. Remove cover, stir, cover, and cook for another 5 minutes. Repeat this process until the onions are limp and beginning to brown. Stir in vinegar, Worcestershire sauce, and black pepper. Add broth and bring to a boil. Reduce heat, cover, and cook for another 30 minutes. To serve, ladle the soup into bowls, top with croutons, grated Parmesan cheese, and shredded mozzarella.

Note: This soup is special enough to serve to company and easy enough for a quick, satisfying meal before a night of running kids to activities. Don't be afraid to serve this to your kids—my picky kids, (who normally won't go near onions) LOVE it and even REQUEST it!

Reuben Sandwiches

Ingredients: Per person: 2 slices rye bread; ¼ lb. thinly sliced deli corned beef; 1 slice Swiss cheese; ¼ cup sauerkraut; 1 Tbsp. Thousand Island dressing.

Directions: Preheat a Foreman grill (or a pancake griddle). Drain sauerkraut and heat on the grill for 3-5 minutes; remove and set aside. Place corned beef on the grill and heat for 3-5 minutes; remove and set aside. Place ½ of the rye bread on the grill. Layer the bread with sauerkraut, meat, and cheese. Top with remaining rye bread slices that have been spread with Thousand Island dressing. Close grill and cook for about 2 minutes. Remove, cut in half, and serve.

Day 2

Creamy Chicken Cordon Bleu in a crock pot:

Ingredients: 6 boneless, skinless chicken breasts; 6 slices Swiss cheese; 6 slices deli ham; 1 large onion, diced; 1 clove garlic, minced; 1 large can (or 2 small cans) cream of chicken soup; 1 can chicken broth; 1 tsp. parsley.

Directions: Place chicken breasts between 2 layers of waxed paper and pound (I usually use a coffee cup since I don't have a meat mallet). Place ham and cheese on the inside of the chicken breast and roll. You can secure with toothpicks if you want, but I usually don't. Place seam side down in the crock pot. In a mixing bowl, mix the soup, broth, onion, garlic, and parsley together. Pour over chicken rolls. Cook on low for 6-8 hours.

Brown rice pilaf:

Ingredients: 3 cups brown rice; ½ lb. fresh mushrooms, sliced; 1 small onion, diced; 3 tsp. butter; small bag slivered almonds; 1 tsp. salt; 6 cups water.

Directions: Melt butter. Add onion and mushrooms; cook for about 2 minutes. Add remaining ingredients. Bring to a boil and simmer for about 40 minutes. Fluff with a fork.

Peas:

Ingredients: Frozen peas; 1 Tbsp. butter; salt and pepper.

Directions: Heat peas according to package directions. Stir in butter. Add salt and pepper to taste.

Day 3

Tacos:

Ingredients: 2 lbs. ground beef; 1 large onion, diced; 1 envelope taco seasoning; 1 Tbsp. chili powder; 1 tsp. ground cumin; 1 can Spicy V-8 juice; 1 can diced tomatoes with green chilies.

Directions: Brown ground beef and diced onions; drain. Add remaining ingredients. Simmer for about 30 minutes. Serve in taco shells with lettuce, tomato, shredded cheese, and sour cream.

Refried bean dip:

Ingredients: 2 cans refried beans; 1 can diced tomatoes with green chilies; 1 envelope taco seasoning mix; sour cream; shredded cheddar cheese.

Directions: Mash first 3 ingredients together and spread into a 9x11 inch pan. Bake at 350 degrees for about 20 minutes. Remove from oven and top with sour cream and cheese. Serve with tortilla chips.

Fresh Salsa:

Ingredients: 2 cans (4 oz. each) chopped green chilies; 4 tomatoes, chopped; 3 green onions, sliced; 2 Tbsp. minced fresh cilantro; 1 jalapeno pepper, seeded and minced (protect your hands with rubber gloves when handling jalapenos!); 1 garlic clove, minced; ⅓ cup red wine vinegar; ⅓ cup olive oil; 1 tsp. ground cumin; 1 tsp. salt; 2 tsp. chili powder; ½ tsp. black pepper.

Directions: In a bowl, combine chilies, tomatoes, cilantro, jalapeno, and garlic. In a jar with a tight-fitting lid (like a Mason jar), combine vinegar, oil, salt, pepper, cumin, and chili powder. Shake jar vigorously. Add the contents of the jar to the bowl of vegetables. Stir to combine. Cover and chill for at least 2 hours.
Note: you can make this the night before to really bring out the flavors!

Day 4

Taco salad:

Ingredients: Leftover taco meat, refried bean dip, and salsa from Day 3; iceberg lettuce, torn; Fritos chili cheese chips; Catalina dressing; shredded cheddar cheese; sour cream.

Directions: Combine and reheat leftover taco meat and refried beans. For each serving, top a large plate with torn lettuce, Fritos, meat mixture, salsa, cheese, sour cream, and Catalina dressing.
Note: depending on how much salsa you have leftover, you may need to use more or less of the Catalina dressing.

Day 5

Blueberry Pancakes:

Ingredients: 1 box blueberry muffin mix; 2 cups Bisquick mix; 2 cups milk; 3 eggs; ¼ cup oil.

Directions: Drain and set the tins of blueberries aside. Mix blueberry muffin mix and Bisquick. Make a well in the center and add oil, eggs, and milk. Stir well. Add more milk or Bisquick until your desired consistency for the batter is reached. Gently stir in the tins of blueberries. Spray a large skillet or griddle with cooking spray and heat until a drop of water can sizzle on the surface. Use a ¼ measuring cup to scoop and drop batter onto the hot skillet. When edges are dry and bubbles break, flip pancakes.
Note: to keep pancakes warm, I preheat my oven to 250 degrees and then turn it off. I place the pancakes on a baking sheet and pop them into the oven as I continue cooking more pancakes.
Bacon:

Ingredients: 1 lb. sliced bacon

Directions: Preheat a George Foreman grill for 5 minutes. Lay bacon slices on grill and close lid. Check after a few minutes and flip or rearrange slices if necessary. Repeat this process until bacon is crispy. Remove to paper towels when bacon is done.

Day 6

Grilled Italian Chicken Breasts:

Ingredients: 2 family packs boneless, skinless chicken breasts (10-

12 breasts); 1 bottle Italian salad dressing; 2 large sealable storage bags.

Directions: Trim chicken breasts and rinse. Place in plastic bags. Pour ½ the salad dressing in each bag. Squeeze bags to distribute dressing over chicken. Marinate 2 hours or more. Remove from bag; discard bags and marinade. Grill on a gas or charcoal grill over medium heat until meat thermometer reads 180 degrees.

Herbed vegetables:

Ingredients: 1 small head cauliflower, cut into florets; 1 bunch broccoli, cut into florets; 2 medium zucchini, sliced; 1 onion, cut into wedges; 2 medium tomatoes, cut into wedges; ½ lb. mushrooms, sliced; 1 stick butter, cubed; 1 tsp. dried thyme; 1 tsp. dried parsley; 1 tsp. dried basil; ½ tsp. dried oregano;1 tsp. garlic salt; ⅓ cup grated Parmesan cheese.

Directions: On a large round microwave-safe platter, arrange the cauliflower, broccoli, zucchini, onion, and mushrooms. Cover with waxed paper and microwave on high 7 minutes; drain. While the veggies are cooking, combine butter, herbs, and garlic salt in a small saucepan. Cook until the butter is melted. Stir well. Arrange the tomatoes on the platter with the other vegetables. Drizzle butter mixture over vegetables; sprinkle with Parmesan cheese. Cook the vegetables uncovered, on high for 2 minutes.

Garlic breadsticks:

Ingredients: 1¼ cups wheat bread flour; 2 tsp. sugar; 1 ½ tsp. baking powder; ½ tsp. salt; ⅔ cup milk; 3 Tbsp. butter, melted; garlic salt.

Directions: Combine flour, sugar, baking powder, and salt. Gradually add milk and stir to form soft dough. Turn onto a floured surface; knead gently 3-4 times. Roll into a 10-in. x 5 in. x ½ in. rectangle. Cut into 12 breadsticks. Pour the melted butter into a 13-in. x 9 in. x 2 in. baking pan. Place the breadsticks in the butter and turn to coat. Sprinkle with garlic salt. Bake at 450 degrees for 14-18 minutes or until golden brown.

Day 7

Chicken Alfredo:

Ingredients: Leftover chicken and herbed vegetables from Day 6; 2 jars Alfredo sauce; 2 packages fettuccini noodles; cracked black pepper; grated Parmesan cheese.

Directions: Fill a large pot with water. Add a little salt and olive oil (about a tsp. each) to the water and bring to a boil. While waiting for the water to boil, dice leftover chicken; place in a large sauté pan. Add leftover vegetables to the chicken and heat through. Pour Alfredo sauce over chicken and vegetables and continue heating. Cook noodles according to package directions. Drain and return to the cooking pot. Pour Alfredo sauce mixture over the noodles and toss gently with a pasta server. Top each serving with pepper and Parmesan cheese.

Week 5

29. Chicken with hot pepper cheese
    a. Spicy rice
    b. Cool cucumbers

30. Ground beef gyros (uses leftover cucumbers from Day 1)
    a. Greek salad

31. Spaghetti with meat sauce (uses leftover meat from Day 2)
    a. Sautéed zucchini
    b. Garlic bread

32. Beer brats
    a. Sweet broccoli salad
    b. Sour cream and chive potato casserole

33. Hawaiian chicken in a crock pot
    a. Brown rice with snow peas and water chestnuts

34. Potato soup
    a. Stromboli

35. No-peek beef
    a. Mashed potatoes
    b. Italian green beans

Shopping List for Week 5

6 large cucumbers
32 oz. sour cream
8 oz. hot pepper cheese
1 envelope taco seasoning mix
2 (4 oz.) cans diced green chilies
1 (16 oz.) dark red kidney beans
1 Garlic bulb
Whole wheat pita bread (4-6 pitas)
Salad greens (like Romaine)
1 (6 oz.) jar pitted black olives
1 green pepper
1 (15 oz.) can diced tomatoes
1 (3 oz.) can Italian tomato paste
2 (15 oz.) cans tomato sauce
2 lbs. wheat blend spaghetti noodles
2 medium yellow squash
2 pkgs. brats (about 8-10)
1 lb. baby carrots
Soy sauce
1 envelope dry onion soup mix
2 (8 oz.) cheddar cheese
2 (16 oz.) Italian green beans
Dry roasted salted peanuts (sm. can)
20 oz. can pineapple tidbits
6 oz. can sliced water chestnuts
2 tubes refrigerated crusty French loaf
1 lg. can cream of mushroom soup
2 envelopes dry Italian salad dressing mix
1 (10½ oz.) can cream of chicken soup
3 lbs. beef stew meat (or get a roast and cube it up)

Yeast
8 oz. plain yogurt
2 bottles dark beer
3 lbs. onions
1 lb. brown rice
2 fresh jalapenos
2 lbs. ground beef
½ cup feta cheese
2 tomatoes
1 red onion
Dijon mustard
½ lb. deli ham
½ lb. deli salami
1 red bell pepper
1 pkg. hot dog buns
2 medium zucchini
Fresh garlic chives
1 32 oz. jar sauerkraut
8 oz. mozzarella
1 bunch celery
Carrots
2 bunches broccoli
1 cup raisins
½ lb. fresh snow peas
10 lbs. potatoes

1 large package frozen shredded hash brown potatoes
10-12 boneless, skinless chicken breasts
2 bottles dark beer (I like Amberbock)
6 (10½ oz.) cans low sodium chicken broth
Seasoned dry bread crumbs

Recipes for Week 5

Day 1

Chicken with hot pepper cheese:

Ingredients: 6 boneless, skinless chicken breasts pounded between 2 sheets of waxed paper to within ½ inch; 8 oz. hot pepper cheese, cut into sticks; 1 envelope taco seasoning; 1 cup seasoned dry bread crumbs; 1 can diced green chilies.

Directions: In a pie plate, mix bread crumbs and taco seasoning. Place a cheese stick and about a tablespoon of green chilies on each chicken breast. Tuck ends of chicken in and roll up, securing with a toothpick (don't forget you have toothpicks in there!). Carefully roll chicken in crumb mixture. Place in a greased baking dish. Bake the chicken uncovered, at 350 degrees for 35-40 minutes or until chicken reads 180 degrees with a meat thermometer.

Spicy Rice Pilaf

Ingredients: 2 cups brown rice; 4 cups water or chicken broth; 1 can diced green chilies; 2 fresh jalapeños, seeded and chopped (use rubber gloves!); 1 large onion, diced; 1 can dark red kidney beans; 1 tsp. cumin; 2 tsp. chili powder; 2 tsp. butter.

Directions: Melt the butter in a large saucepan. Add onions and jalapenos. Cook and stir until onions become translucent. Add remaining ingredients. Bring to a boil, then turn down heat and simmer 40 minutes. Fluff with a fork.

Cool Cucumbers:

Ingredients: 1 cup sour cream; 1 cup plain yogurt; ½ red onion, sliced; 4 Tbsp. lemon juice; 4 Tbsp. red wine vinegar; 5 large cucumbers, peeled, seeded, and thinly sliced; 1 clove garlic, minced.

Directions: In a salad bowl, combine sour cream, yogurt, lemon juice, and vinegar. Add onion, garlic, and cucumber slices; mix well. Chill for at least 1 hour. (You will use the leftovers from this salad tomorrow.)

Day 2

Ground beef gyros:

Ingredients: Leftover cucumber salad; 2 lbs. ground beef; 1 large onion, diced; 2 cloves garlic, minced; 1 tsp. salt; 1 tsp. pepper; 2 tsp. oregano; 2 tsp. basil; wheat pita bread pockets; leftover cool cucumbers from Day 1.

Directions: Brown ground beef, onion, garlic, and herbs. Drain. Place cucumber salad in the blender and blend. Fill pita shells and top with cucumber sauce.

Greek salad:

Ingredients: 12 cups torn salad greens; 2 tomatoes, cut into wedges; 1 medium cucumber, peeled, seeded, and sliced; ½ medium green pepper, sliced; ½ red onion, sliced; ½ cup black olives; ½ cup crumbled feta cheese; croutons, if desired.

Directions: Toss well in a large salad bowl. Top with lemon-herb dressing and toss again.

Lemon-herb dressing:

Ingredients: ¼ cup olive oil; 2 Tbsp. lemon juice; 2 tsp. Dijon mustard; 2 garlic cloves, minced; ½ tsp. oregano; ½ tsp. basil; ¼ tsp. thyme; ¼ tsp. salt; ¼ tsp. pepper.

Directions: Place all ingredients in a jar with a tight-fitting lid (I use a Mason jar). Shake vigorously.

Day 3

Spaghetti with meat sauce (uses meat from Day2):

Ingredients: Leftover meat from ground beef gyros; 1 can diced tomatoes; 1 can Italian tomato paste; 2 (15 oz.) cans tomato sauce; 1 tsp. basil; 1 tsp. parsley; 1 tsp. oregano; 1 tsp. garlic powder; spaghetti noodles.

Directions: Combine all ingredients. Bring to a boil and then simmer for at least 30 minutes. Cook spaghetti according to package directions. Serve sauce over hot spaghetti noodles.

Garlic bread:

Ingredients: 1 cup plus 3 Tbsp. hot water; 5 tsp. butter; 1 tsp. garlic salt; 1 envelope dry Italian dressing mix; 1 Tbsp. sugar; 3 cups wheat bread flour; 4 ½ tsp. nonfat dry milk powder; 2 ¼ tsp. active dry yeast.

Directions: In a bread machine pan, place all ingredients in the order listed above. Select the "basic" setting. Bake according to bread machine directions.

Sautéed zucchini:

Ingredients: 2 medium yellow squash, sliced; 2 medium zucchini, sliced; 1 red bell pepper, diced; ¼ cup olive oil; 1 envelope dry Italian salad dressing; 3 Tbsp. red wine vinegar.

Directions: In a skillet over medium-high heat, stir fry the vegetables for about 4 minutes. Sprinkle with salad dressing and vinegar; mix well and serve.

Day 4

Beer brats:

Ingredients: 2 packages brats; 1 large onion, sliced; 1 jar sauerkraut, drained; 2 bottles dark beer.

Directions: Mix all ingredients in a large pan. Bring to a boil then simmer for 2-3 hours. Preheat Foreman grill or outdoor grill. Carefully remove brats from onion-kraut mixture and grill until the skins are crispy. Serve with mustard, and reserved onion-kraut mixture on a hotdog bun.

Sweet broccoli salad:

Ingredients: 2 bunches of broccoli, cut into florets; 1 cup peanuts; 1 cup raisins; ½ cup chopped onion; 1 cup Miracle Whip salad dressing; 2 Tbsp. red wine vinegar; 2 Tbsp. sugar.

Directions: In a salad bowl, combine broccoli, peanuts, raisins, and onions. In a small bowl, combine salad dressing, vinegar, and sugar. Pour over vegetables and toss to coat. Cover and refrigerate for at least 1 hour before serving.

Sour cream and chive potato casserole:

Ingredients: 1 package frozen shredded hash browns, thawed; 1 small onion, diced; 16 oz. sour cream; cream of chicken soup; 1 stick butter, melted; 1 cup cheddar cheese, shredded; ½ cup fresh garlic chives, minced.

Directions: In a large bowl, combine all ingredients. Transfer to a large greased casserole dish. Cover and bake at 350 degrees for 30 minutes. Remove cover and bake 15 minutes longer.

Day 5

Hawaiian chicken in a crock pot:

Ingredients: 1 lb. baby carrots; ½ a green bell pepper, slices; 1 medium onion, cut into wedges; 6 boneless, skinless chicken breasts; 1 can (20 oz.) pineapple tidbits; 1 garlic clove, minced; ⅓ cup brown sugar; ⅓ cup soy sauce; 1 tsp. ground ginger.

Directions: In a crock pot, layer carrots, green pepper, onion, and garlic. Top with the chicken. Drain pineapple, reserving juice. Pour juice into a small bowl. Add brown sugar, soy sauce and ginger to the juice and stir to combine. Pour over pineapple. Cover and cook on low for 7-8 hours. Serve over brown rice with snow peas and water chestnuts.

Brown rice with snow peas and water chestnuts:

Ingredients: 2 cups brown rice; ½ lb. fresh snow peas; 4 cups water; 1 can sliced water chestnuts, drained and rinsed; 2 tsp. butter; 1 Tbsp. soy sauce.
Directions: Melt butter in a saucepan; add rice and water. Bring to a boil and simmer 20 minutes. Add water chestnuts, snow peas, and soy sauce. Simmer 20 minutes more.

Note: you can also add fresh mushrooms to this rice dish, but I'm usually pushing my luck to get my picky eaters to eat the snow peas!

Day 6

Potato soup:

Ingredients: 2 onions, diced; 4 carrots, peeled and sliced; 10 potatoes, peeled and diced; 2 or 3 ribs celery, sliced; ¼ cup of butter; 4 cans chicken broth; 2 cups milk; 1 tsp. salt; 1 tsp. pepper; 1 tsp. paprika .

Directions: Melt butter in a large pot. Add onions, carrots, and celery. Cook and stir for about 5 minutes. Add seasonings, potatoes, and broth. Be sure to have the potatoes covered with liquid (you might need to add more chicken broth or some water). Bring to a boil and cook until veggies are tender. Mash veggies with a potato masher or pastry blender. Add milk and heat through. Sprinkle with additional paprika, if desired.

Stromboli:

Ingredients: 2 tubes (11 oz.) each Pillsbury Crusty French Loaf Bread; 2 cups shredded mozzarella cheese; 2 cups cheddar cheese; ½ lb. deli ham; ½ lb. deli salami; 2 Tbsp. butter, melted; grated Parmesan cheese.

Directions: Unroll each tube of dough and spread each on a greased baking sheet so that you have a large rectangle of dough on each. Sprinkle each with 1 cup mozzarella and 1 cup cheddar cheese; top each with ½ the ham and salami. Carefully roll up, jelly-roll style, starting with the short side. Seal the seams and tuck the ends under. Brush with butter and sprinkle with Parmesan cheese. Bake at 350 degrees for 25-30 minutes. Slice with a serrated knife.

Day 7

No-peek beef:

Ingredients: 3 lbs. beef stew meat (or a roast cut into bite-sized portions); 1 large can cream of mushroom soup; 1 envelope dry onion soup mix; 1 tsp. pepper.
Directions: Mix all ingredients together in a large covered casserole. Cover with lid. Bake at 350 degrees for 3 hours. Don't peek!

Mashed potatoes

Ingredients: 5 lbs potatoes; salt and pepper to taste; 3/4 cup (or so) milk; 1 stick butter.

Directions: Add 2 tsp. salt to a large pot of water. Bring it to a boil. While the water is heating, wash and peel about 5 pounds of potatoes.

You can leave the peel on half of them if you want more fiber and texture. Dice the potatoes and put them in the boiling water. Boil until fork-tender (20-30 minutes). Drain potatoes in a colander. While the potatoes are draining, place a stick of butter in the bottom of the pot you cooked it in if you are using a hand mixer or in the bottom of the bowl of your standing mixer. Mash potatoes until large lumps are gone, add milk, salt, and pepper, and then mash until smooth.

Italian Green Beans:

Ingredients: 2 16 oz. cans Italian green beans, drained; 1 small onion, diced; 1 Tbsp. olive oil, 1 clove garlic, minced; ½ tsp. dried basil; ½ tsp. dried oregano; salt and pepper to taste.

Directions: Heat oil in a sauté pan. Add onion and garlic and cook 2 minutes. Turn heat down to medium. Add beans and seasonings. Heat through.

Week 6

36. Breakfast burritos
    a.   Tomato pie

37. Hot Italian subs
    a.   Potato chips

38. Spicy chicken
    a.   Baked potatoes
    b.   Broccoli casserole

39. Chicken fajitas (uses leftover chicken from Day 3)
    a.   Green chile rice

40. Texican chili
    a.   Southwestern corn bread

41. Hamburgers
    a.   Grandma Sandy's macaroni and cheese
    b.   Wilted lettuce and onions

42. Homemade pizza
    a.   Veggies and dip

Shopping List for Week 6

1 Cucumber
1 (8 oz.) can cream-style corn
2 (16 oz.) sour cream
3 (4 oz.) cans diced green chiles
2 (10 oz.) frozen broccoli
1 box cheese flavored croutons
2 (16 oz.) cans pizza sauce
Spicy pizza seasoning (spice aisle)
16 oz. mozzarella
2 lg. cans stewed tomatoes
1 pkg.refrigerated pie crust
8-10 wheat fajita sized tortillas
2 lbs.bacon
½ lb. sandwich size pepperoni
½ lb. deli turkey
8 oz. sliced provolone cheese
1 jar banana pepper rings
3 or 4 asst. color bell peppers
Fresh garlic chives
3 lbs. beef stew meat
4 boxes macaroni and cheese
1 envelope dry ranch dressing mix
1 kg. hamburger buns
1 garlic bulb
1 (16 oz.) can kidney beans
2 (28 oz.) cans stewed tomatoes
10-12 boneless, skinless chicken breasts
2 (10 ½ oz.) cans of cream of broccoli soup

1 head cauliflower
Cornmeal
10 lbs. potatoes
8 oz. hot pepper cheese
16 oz. cheddar cheese
1 pkg. sub buns
8 oz. pepperoni
1 head green leaf lettuce
1 head broccoli
2 lbs. carrots
4 pre-made pizza crusts
8-10 burrito sized tortillas
1 bag potato chips
1 lb. deli ham
8 oz. sliced Colby cheese
4 fresh medium tomatoes
1 bunch green onion
2 dozen eggs
Saltine crackers
1 red onion
1 lb. spaghetti noodles
1 ½ lbs. ground beef
1 lb. butter
1 lb. brown rice
2 (8 oz.) cans tomato sauce
3 lbs. beef stew meat

Recipes for Week 6

Day 1

Breakfast Burritos:

Ingredients: 10 flour tortillas; 16 eggs; 3 green onions, sliced; 1 lb. bacon (½ will be used for tomato pie); ½ stick butter; salt and pepper to taste; 1 cup shredded cheddar cheese; salsa, if desired.

Directions: Fry bacon or grill on a Foreman grill; cool and dice. You will use ½ of the bacon for the burritos and use the other ½ for the tomato pie. Melt butter in a large pan. Add green onions, eggs, and salt and pepper; scramble eggs until set. Add cheese and bacon, stir to combine. Place about ½ cup in a flour tortilla, fold ends in and roll. Serve with salsa, if desired.
Note: save a couple Tbsp. of the bacon drippings for the wilted lettuce on Day 6; just put it in a small covered dish and refrigerate.

Tomato pie:

Ingredients: 4 medium sized tomatoes, sliced; 2 Tbsp. fresh garlic chives, minced; ½ lb. bacon, cooked and diced; 1 pie crust; 1 cup cheddar cheese, shredded; ¾ cup Miracle Whip salad dressing.

Directions: Pre-bake pie crust according to package directions. Layer tomato slices, chives, and bacon. In a bowl, mix Miracle Whip and shredded cheese. Spread Miracle Whip mixture to within 2 inches of the perimeter of the pie. Bake at 350 degrees for 35 minutes. Cool 5 minutes before slicing.

Day 2

Hot Italian subs:

Ingredients: 1 lb. deli ham; ½ lb. deli turkey; ½ lb. deli sandwich pepperoni; red onion, sliced; pickled banana pepper slices; 8 oz. sliced Colby cheese; 8 oz. sliced provolone cheese; pizza sauce; sub buns.

Directions: For each sandwich, spread pizza sauce on the inside of the bottom and top sub bun. Layer the ham, pepperoni, provolone, turkey, banana peppers, red onion, and provolone cheese on the sub bun. Bake at 350 degrees for 10 minutes. Serve with your family's favorite potato chips.

Day 3

Spicy chicken:

Ingredients: Angie's spice rub; 10-12 boneless chicken breasts.

Directions: Trim visible fat from chicken; rinse and pat dry. Place 3 chicken breasts in a large plastic container with a lid. Sprinkle with 1 Tbsp. spice rub. Cover container with lid and shake to coat chicken. Place chicken in a large foil roasting/ grilling bag. Repeat until all chicken is seasoned. Bake at 450 degrees for 45 minutes. Let stand in foil 10 minutes before opening foil.
*Note: You can make this chicken on the grill (5-7 minutes per side) and then cover it in foil for 10 minutes or bake it on a sided cookie sheet covered with foil. Leaving it sit for 10 minutes in the foil seems to bring out the juices. Also, you can adjust the amount of seasoning to your family's tastes. If you really want it hot, marinate the chicken in the spices for an hour or more before cooking.

Baked potatoes:

Ingredients: 6 large potatoes; spray oil; foil; salt and pepper to taste; butter and sour cream.
Directions: Scrub potatoes and prick in several places with a fork. Lay each potato on a square of foil and spray with oil; roll potato up in the foil. Bake at 450 degrees for 45 minutes to an hour. Top with salt, pepper, butter, and sour cream.

Broccoli casserole:

Ingredients: 2 (10 oz.) packages frozen broccoli, thawed; 2 cans cream of broccoli soup; ½ cup sour cream; ½ stick butter, melted; 1 cup crushed croutons; 1 cup shredded cheddar cheese.

Directions: In a large bowl, mix soup, sour cream, and cheese. Add broccoli and mix well. Transfer to a greased casserole dish. Top with crouton crumbs and drizzle with melted butter. Cover and bake at 450 degrees for 30 minutes, removing the cover for the last 5 minutes of cook-time.

Day 4

Chicken fajitas (uses leftover chicken from Day 3):

Ingredients: Leftover spicy chicken; red onion; 3 or 4 assorted colored bell peppers; wheat fajita tortillas; 1 Tbsp. oil; salsa.

Directions: Slice chicken into strips. Slice vegetables. Heat the oil in a large sauté pan. Add vegetables and stir fry for about 5 minutes. Add chicken and continue cooking until the chicken is heated through. While the chicken is cooking, warm the wheat tortillas by placing them, one at a time, over a hot burner; turn with tongs to heat both sides. Place chicken and vegetable mixture in wheat tortillas and top with salsa.

Green chile rice:

Ingredients: 4 cups cooked brown rice; 2 (4 oz.) cans chopped green chiles; 1 tsp. salt; 8 oz. hot pepper cheese, cut into cubes; 16 oz. sour cream.

Directions: Make rice according to the package directions; place in a large bowl. Add remaining ingredients to the rice; stir well. Transfer to a greased 2 quart baking dish. Cover and bake for 30 minutes.

Day 5

Texican chili:

Ingredients: 8 bacon strips, diced; 3 lbs. beef stew meat, cut into bite-sized pieces; 2 (28 oz.) cans stewed tomatoes; 2 (8oz.) cans tomato sauce; 1 can kidney beans, drained and rinsed; 2 cups sliced carrots; 1 onion, diced; 1 cup sliced celery; 1 Tbsp. parsley, 2 Tbsp. chili powder; 1 tsp. cumin; 1 tsp. pepper.

Directions: In a skillet, cook bacon until crisp, remove to paper towel to drain. Brown the beef in bacon drippings. Transfer beef, bacon, and remaining ingredients to a crock pot; stir well. Cover and cook on low 9-10 hours.

Southwestern corn bread:

Ingredients: 1 cup yellow cornmeal; 1 Tbsp. baking powder; 1 cup cream-style corn; ¾ tsp. salt; 1 cup sour cream; ⅔ cup butter; melted; 2 eggs; 1 cup shredded cheddar cheese; 1 can diced green chiles.

Directions: In a bowl, combine cornmeal, baking powder, and salt. Combine remaining ingredients in another bowl. Add wet ingredients to dry ingredients and stir until blended. Pour into a greased 9 inch square baking pan. Bake at 350 degrees for 1 hour.

Day 6

Hamburgers:

Ingredients: 1 ½ lbs. ground chuck; 1 Tbsp. steak seasoning; 2 Tbsp. ketchup; 1 Tbsp. Worcestershire sauce; wheat hamburger buns; lettuce; tomato; sliced red onion; and your favorite condiments.
Directions: In a large bowl, thoroughly mix meat, steak seasoning, ketchup, and Worcestershire sauce. Shape into patties. Either grill outside on a gas or charcoal grill or indoors on a George Foreman grill until burgers are well done. Serve on wheat hamburger buns with lettuce, tomato, onions, and condiments of your choice.

Grandma Sandy's macaroni and cheese:

Ingredients: 16 oz. box spaghetti noodles, cooked according to package directions and drained; the cheese powder from 4 boxes macaroni and cheese (save the elbows for another use); 1 sleeve saltine crackers, crushed; 2 sticks butter; milk (about a quart); salt and pepper.

Directions: Spray a large glass casserole (including the underside of the lid) liberally with cooking oil. Put a layer of spaghetti noodles in the bottom of the dish, sprinkle with salt, pepper, and powdered cheese, cracker crumbs, more cheese, and dot with butter. Repeat layers, ending up with a layer of cheese on top. Pour milk over all. Take a butter knife and poke it through the layers and wiggle it. Do this all over the casserole to distribute the milk. You may need to add more milk. Cover and bake at 300 degrees for 2 ½ – 3 hours. The top and sides will be browned, but not burned.

Wilted lettuce and onions:

Ingredients: 1 head leaf lettuce, torn; 2-3 Tbsp. bacon drippings; 3 green onions, sliced; 2 Tbsp. sugar; 2 Tbsp. cider vinegar.

Directions: Place lettuce in a large salad bowl. In a pan, melt bacon drippings. Add onion and cook 2 minutes. Turn off heat and add sugar and vinegar. Mix well. Pour over lettuce and toss thoroughly.

Day 7

Homemade pizza:

Ingredients: 4 prepared pizza crusts; 1 can pizza sauce; 8 oz. pepperoni; sliced onion, 16 oz. mozzarella cheese (shredded); garlic powder; fresh mushrooms; 1 sm. jar sliced black olives; 1 sm. jar sliced green olives; banana peppers.

Directions: Heat oven to 375 degrees. Spray pizza crusts with oil. Bake (2 at a time) for 5 minutes. Spread each pizza crust with ¼ of pizza sauce. Sprinkle with garlic powder. Top each pizza with 1 cup cheese, ¼ of the pepperoni, mushrooms, onions, and your desired amount of drained olives and banana peppers. Bake 2 pizzas at a time for 10-15 minutes.

Veggies and dip

Ingredients: Carrots; celery; cucumber; broccoli, cauliflower; 1 pint sour cream; 1 packet dry ranch dressing mix.

Directions: Peel and wash veggies. Cut carrots and celery into sticks. Slice cucumber. Chop broccoli and cauliflower into florets. Mix sour cream and dry ranch dressing mix together with a fork.

Week 7

43. Lasagna
    a.   Garlic bread
    b.   Tossed salad

44. Hot dogs
    a.   Baked beans
    b.   Cole slaw

45. Chicken enchiladas
    a.   Sliced cucumbers and tomatoes

46. Beef and bean pie
    a.   Frozen mixed corn

47. Meatball stew
    a.   Biscuits

48. Chicken drumsticks
    a.   Roasted potatoes
    b.   Celery sticks and bleu cheese dressing

49. BBQ pork chops
    a.   Pepper cheese scalloped potatoes
    b.   Hot bean salad

Shopping List for Week 7

1 (10 oz.) pkg. frozen creamed corn
BBQ sauce
1 pkg. hot dog buns
1 envelope dry onion soup mix
8 oz. cheddar cheese
2 lg. cans baked beans
2 lbs. carrots
8-10 wheat fajita sized tortillas
1 envelope taco seasoning mix
Salad vegetables (your choice)
1(10 ½ oz.) cream of chicken soup
2 (16 oz.) cans refried beans
1 pkg. of 2 refrigerated pie crust
12-16 chicken drumsticks
Blue cheese salad dressing
16 oz. wheat lasagna noodles
3 (1 ½ lb.) packages ground beef
1 family size can tomato soup
1(10 ½ oz.) bean with bacon soup
2 (16 oz.) cans kidney beans
1 (28 oz.) can tomato purée
1 (16 oz.) black beans
1 (16 oz.) green beans
1 (16 oz.) garbanzo beans
6-8 boneless, skinless chicken breasts
1 (10 oz.) pkg. frozen corn in butter sauce
2 (15 oz.) cans diced tomatoes with green chiles
16 oz. sour cream

Baking mix (like Bisquick)
1 pkg. hot dogs
8 oz. hot pepper cheese
10 lbs. potatoes
16 oz. mozzarella
1 sm. green cabbage
1 red onion
Salsa
2 lbs. red potatoes
1 bunch celery
Salad greens (like romaine)
2 tomatoes
8 oz. ricotta cheese
1 lb. bacon
2 (16 oz.) tomato sauce
6-8 boneless pork chops
1 lb. bulk Italian sausage
1 garlic bulb
Grated Parmesan cheese
2 cucumbers
2 (6 oz.) tomato paste
1 bunch green onions
1 (8 oz.) can wax beans

Recipes for Week 7

Day 1

Lasagna:

Ingredients: 16 oz. wheat lasagna noodles; 1 ½ lbs. ground beef; 1 lb. bulk Italian sausage; 3-4 cloves garlic cloves, minced; 2 onions, diced; tomato paste; 2 (16 oz.) cans tomato sauce; 1 large can tomato puree; 2 (8oz.) bars mozzarella cheese, shredded; ½ cup grated Parmesan cheese; 8 oz. ricotta cheese; 2 eggs; 1 Tbsp. parsley flakes; 1 Tbsp. basil; 2 tsp. oregano; 2 tsp. thyme.

Directions: Brown ground beef, Italian sausage, garlic, and onions. Drain and place in a large pot. Add tomato paste; 2 (16 oz.) cans tomato sauce; 1 large can tomato puree; 1 Tbsp. basil; 2 tsp. oregano; 2 tsp. thyme. Bring to a boil, and then simmer at least 1 hour. Meanwhile, bring a large pot of water to a boil. Add one tsp. each oil and salt to the water. When the water comes to a boil, add the noodles and cook according to package directions. Drain noodles and then rinse with cold water. In a medium sized bowl, combine parsley, eggs, Parmesan, and ricotta. Remove the meat sauce from the heat. Into a large, greased casserole dish; ladle about a cup of meat sauce and spread it around. Lay noodles across the bottom of the dish and make a ring of noodles around the sides of the dish. Begin layering ingredients in the following order: meat sauce, ricotta, mozzarella, and noodles. Continue layering until casserole dish is full. Top with sauce. (If you have any sauce left, put it in a freezer bag and use it the next time you make spaghetti.) Cover the lasagna with foil. Place casserole on a large jellyroll pan and bake at 350 degrees for 1 hour, and then remove foil and cook for another 15 minutes. Allow to stand for about 10 minutes before cutting into it.

Garlic bread:

Ingredients: ¾ cup plus 2 Tbsp. water; 2 Tbsp. butter; 1 tsp. salt; 3 cups bread flour; ¼ cup nonfat dry milk powder; 2 tsp. garlic powder; 4 tsp. sugar; 2 tsp. yeast.

Directions: Add ingredients to your bread machine in the order listed above. Set the bread machine to the basic/white bread cycle.

Tossed salad:

Ingredients: Salad greens, washed and torn; salad vegetables, such as sliced carrots, sliced celery, sliced cucumbers, and grape tomatoes; your favorite salad dressing; croutons.

Directions: Toss salad greens and veggies. Top with your favorite salad dressing and croutons.

Day 2

Hot dogs:

Ingredients: 1 package hot dogs; hot dog buns; diced onion; ketchup, mustard, and relish.

Directions: Grill hotdogs to desired doneness on an outdoor grill or George Foreman grill. Place hot dog in a bun and top with diced onion; ketchup, mustard, and relish.

Baked beans:

Ingredients: 2 cans baked beans, pork fat removed;   cup brown sugar; 2 Tbsp. cider vinegar;   cup ketchup; 1 tsp. ground mustard; 3 strips of bacon.
Directions: In a greased casserole dish, combine all ingredients except bacon. Lay bacon strips on top and bake for 45 minutes at 350 degrees.

Cole slaw:

Ingredients: 1 head cabbage, shredded; 1 red onion, diced; 3 carrots, peeled and shredded; 2 Tbsp. red wine vinegar; 2 Tbsp. sugar; 1 cup Miracle Whip salad dressing; ½ tsp. salt; ½ tsp. pepper.

Directions: In a small mixing bowl, mix vinegar, sugar, salt, pepper, and Miracle Whip. Place cabbage, onion, and carrots in a salad bowl. Top with dressing and toss to coat. Cover and chill for at least ½ an hour.

Day 3

Chicken enchiladas:

Ingredients: 6-8 boneless, skinless chicken breasts; 1 envelope taco seasoning mix; 2 cans diced tomatoes with green chilies; 1 can cream of chicken soup; 10 burrito shells; 2 cans refried beans; 1 cup salsa; 1 ½ cups shredded cheddar cheese; sour cream.

Directions: Trim visible fat from chicken; rinse and pat dry. Place chicken in a crock pot and sprinkle with taco seasoning mix. Pour diced tomatoes and soup over chicken. Stir it around a bit. Cook on low for 6 hours. Shred chicken with forks. Spread about a ½ cup of chicken mixture in a burrito shell, tuck ends in and roll. Place seam side down in a lasagna pan. Repeat until chicken mixture is used up. (If you have any extra chicken mixture, you can spread it over the burrito shells.) In a medium bowl, combine the refried beans and salsa. Spread over chicken. Bake at 350 degrees for 30-30 minutes. Top with shredded cheese and sour cream.

Sliced cucumbers and tomatoes:

Ingredients: 2 tomatoes; 2 cucumbers; salt.

Directions: Peel and slice cucumbers. Slice tomatoes. Arrange in a circular pattern on a plate. Sprinkle with salt, if desired.

Day 4

Beef and bean pie:

Ingredients: 1 lb ground beef; 2 or 3 garlic cloves, minced; 1 can bean with bacon soup (undiluted); 2 cups salsa, divided; 1 Tbsp. cornstarch; 1 tsp. parsley; 1 tsp. salt; 1 tsp. paprika; 1 tsp. chili powder; 1 tsp. pepper; ½ tsp. cumin; 1 can kidney beans, rinsed and drained; 1 can black beans, rinsed and drained; 2 cups shredded cheddar cheese, divided; ¾ cup green onions, divided; pastry for double crust pie (10 inches); sour cream.

Directions: Brown beef and garlic; drain. In a large bowl, combine soup, 1 cup salsa; cornstarch, and spices. Fold in beans, 1 ¼ cup cheese; ½ cup green onions; and beef. Line pie plate with bottom pastry; fill with bean mixture. Top with remaining pastry; seal and flute edges. Cut slits in top crust. Bake the pie at 425 degrees for 30-

35 minutes or until lightly browned. Allow to stand 5 minutes before cutting. Garnish slices with reserved salsa, sour cream, green onion, and cheese.

Mixed frozen corn:

Ingredients: 1 package frozen corn in butter sauce; 1 package frozen creamed corn; salt; and pepper.

Directions: Microwave corn according to package directions. Mix together in a serving dish; salt and pepper to taste.

Day 5

Meatball stew:

Ingredients: 1 ½ lb. ground beef; 1 large can tomato soup; 4 carrots, peeled and sliced; 4 potatoes, peeled and sliced; 2 cups water; 1 envelope dry onion soup mix; ½ cup ketchup; 1 egg; 1 tsp. pepper; 2 beef bouillon cubes; 1 large onion, diced; 2 celery ribs; 2 cloves garlic, minced.

Directions: In a bowl, combine ground beef, dry onion soup mix, ketchup, pepper, garlic, and egg. Form into balls and place on a sided cookie sheet and bake at 350 degrees for 25- 30 minutes. Place the meatballs, potatoes, carrots, onion, and celery in a crock pot. Heat water and dissolve bouillon cubes. Stir tomato soup into bouillon water. Pour over meatballs and vegetables. Cook on low 10 hours.

Biscuits:

Ingredients: 4 ½ baking mix; 1cup milk.

Directions: Heat oven to 450 degrees. In a large mixing bowl, combine ingredients. Sprinkle a little more baking mix on a flat surface. Place the dough on it and knead a few times. Roll dough to ½ inch. Cut with a floured biscuit cutter and place a lightly greased baking sheet. Bake 8-10 minutes or until lightly browned.

Day 6

Chicken Drumsticks:

Ingredients: 1 family pack of chicken drumsticks; Angie's spice rub; 1 stick butter, melted; 2-5 tsp. hot pepper sauce; 2 tsp. garlic salt.

Directions: Place 1 Tbsp. of spice rub in a large plastic bowl that has a lid. Add 3 or 4 drumsticks. Cover with lid and shake to coat. Place drumsticks on a greased jelly roll pan (or cookie sheet with sides). Repeat with remaining drumsticks. Combine butter, garlic salt, and hot pepper sauce; pour over drumsticks. Bake at 375 degrees for 30 minutes; turn and bake for 25 minutes more.

Herb roasted potatoes:

Ingredients: ½ cup whipped salad dressing; 1 envelope dry onion soup mix; ½ cup Italian salad dressing; 2 lbs unpeeled small red potatoes, washed and quartered.

Directions: Mix dressings and onion soup mix in a large bowl. Add potatoes; toss to coat. Place potatoes on a large jellyroll pan that has been coated with cooking spray. Spray more cooking spray over the potatoes. Bake at 350 degrees for 45 minutes to an hour, stirring after 20 minutes. Serve with sour cream for dipping.

Celery and Bleu cheese dressing:

Ingredients: 1 bunch celery; bleu cheese salad dressing.

Directions: Wash and trim celery. Serve with bleu cheese salad dressing for dipping.

Day 7

BBQ pork chops:

Ingredients: 6-8 boneless pork chops; Angie's spice rub; BBQ sauce.

Directions: Rub pork chops with spice rub. Grill 7-8 minutes on each side or until done. Brush with BBQ sauce during the last few minutes. Serve with extra sauce for dipping.

Pepper cheese scalloped potatoes:

Ingredients: 6-8 potatoes, scrubbed and thinly sliced; 1 medium onion, diced; ½ cup butter, melted; ½ tsp. salt; ½ tsp. chili powder; ¼ tsp. cayenne pepper; ¼ tsp. pepper; 2 cups shredded hot pepper cheese.

Directions: Heat oven to 400 degrees. Combine all ingredients in a large bowl. Transfer to a greased casserole and cover. Bake for 50 minutes.

Hot bean salad:

Ingredients: 6 bacon strips, diced; ½ cup sugar; 2 Tbsp. cornstarch; 1 ½ tsp. salt; ½ tsp. pepper; ⅔ cup cider vinegar; ⅓ cup water; 1 can kidney beans, rinsed and drained; 1 can black beans, rinsed and drained; 1 can garbanzo beans, rinsed and drained; 1 can wax beans, rinsed and drained; 1 can green beans, rinsed and drained.

Directions: In a skillet, cook bacon until crisp; reserve ¼ cup drippings. Set bacon aside on paper towels. Add sugar, cornstarch, salt and pepper to drippings. Stir in vinegar and water; bring to a boil, stirring constantly. Cook and stir 2 minutes. Add the beans, reduce heat. Cover and simmer for about 15 minutes or until beans are heated through. Place in a serving bowl; top with bacon.

Week 8

50. Liz's turkey breast
     a. Stuffing
     b. Mashed potatoes with vegetable purée

51. Turkey salad pitas (uses leftover turkey)
     a. Mashed potato soup (uses leftover mashed potatoes)

52. Cincinnati chili spaghetti
     a. Dark green salad with garden herb vinaigrette

53. Bean burritos
     a. Tortilla chips and chili dip (uses leftover chili)

54. Grilled steaks
     a. Broccoli, rice, and bean salad (uses leftover vinaigrette)

55. French onion soup
     a. Reuben sandwiches

56. Lori's quiches
     a. Mixed fresh fruit

Shopping List for Week 8

1 (4-6 lb.) bone-in turkey breast
1 bag herbed stuffing crumbs
2 bunches celery
1 pkg. (4-6) pita bread
1 cup sweetened dried cranberries
1 lb. spaghetti noodles
1 bag fresh baby spinach leaves
1 jar fully cooked bacon bits
Fresh basil
2 (16 oz.) cans refried beans
1 bag tortilla chips
2 (8 oz.) cream cheese
8 oz. strawberry yogurt
16 oz. can kidney beans
8 oz. fresh mushrooms
Grape tomatoes
6 (10 ½ oz.) cans beef broth
1 ½ lbs. deli corned beef
1 loaf rye bread
1 lb. bacon or sausage
Fresh fruit of your choice (4 cups)
Milk
16 oz. cheddar cheese

10 lbs. potatoes
2 lbs. carrots
2 (3 lb.) bags onions

2 lbs. ground beef
15 oz. can tomato sauce
1 bunch green onions
1 cucumber
Fresh oregano
Fresh parsley
Salsa
8-10 wheat burrito shells
1 head fresh broccoli
1 red onion
8 oz. mozzarella
1 lb. Brown rice
Olive oil
8 oz. sliced Swiss cheese
1 jar sauerkraut
8 oz. grape tomatoes
1 dozen eggs
32 oz. jar sauerkraut
Bisquick Baking Mix

6 oz. pkg. chopped walnuts or pecans
Steak (enough for your family; whatever cut you like)
15 oz. can diced tomatoes with green chilies
1 quart can chicken or vegetable broth

Recipes for Week 8

Day 1

Liz's turkey breast:

Ingredients: Bone-in turkey breast, thawed and rinsed; 1 onion, quartered; 2 carrots, peeled and halved, 2 stalks celery, halved; spray oil; 1 cup broth (from quart can); salt and pepper.

Directions: Place turkey breast-side up in a large crock pot. Turn turkey on its side and place vegetables inside the body cavity. Return turkey to first position and sprinkle with salt and pepper. Pour broth into the bottom of the crock pot. Spray turkey with oil. Cook on low for about 8 hours (check for doneness with a meat thermometer, it should read 180). Remove carefully to a serving platter and allow to rest for about 10 minutes before carving.
*Note: this recipe is a combination of 2 recipes from 2 women named Liz.

Mashed potatoes

Ingredients: 5 lbs potatoes; salt and pepper to taste; 3/4 cup (or so) milk; 1 stick butter.

Directions: Add 2 tsp. salt to a large pot of water. Bring it to a boil. While the water is heating, wash and peel about 5 pounds of potatoes. You can leave the peel on half of them if you want more fiber and texture. Dice the potatoes and put them in the boiling water. Boil until fork-tender (20-30 minutes). Drain potatoes in a colander.

While the potatoes are draining, place a stick of butter in the bottom of the pot you cooked it in if you are using a hand mixer or in the bottom of the bowl of your standing mixer. Mash potatoes until large lumps are gone, add milk, salt, and pepper, and then mash until smooth.

Vegetable puree:

Ingredients: Cooked vegetables from the turkey; 1 cup broth/ drippings from the turkey.

Directions: With a slotted spoon, remove vegetables from the crock pot. Place in a blender or food processor. Pulse until pureed. Add 1 cup broth/drippings to puree. Pulse puree and broth until smooth. Pour over mashed potatoes like gravy.

Stuffing:

Ingredients: 1 bag herb seasoned stuffing cubes; 6-8 stalks celery, sliced; 2 onions, chopped; 1 clove garlic; minced; 1 Tbsp. dried parsley; 1 tsp. salt; ½ tsp. pepper; broth (from quart can).

Directions: Spray a shallow casserole dish with cooking oil. In a large bowl, toss all ingredients except broth. Transfer to casserole dish. Pour broth over mixture until well moistened. Bake at 350 degrees until the top is crispy (about 45 minutes).

Day 2

Turkey salad pitas:

Ingredients: Leftover turkey from Day 1, diced or shredded; 2 stalks celery, sliced; 2 green onions, sliced; ¼ cup chopped walnuts or pecans; 1 cup dried sweetened cranberries; Miracle Whip or mayonnaise; salt and pepper to taste; wheat pitas.

Directions: In a large bowl, combine all ingredients except Miracle Whip. The amount of Miracle Whip you use will depend on the amount of turkey you have left. Begin with ½ cup and then add more if you need to. Cut pitas in half (I use kitchen scissors) and fill.

Mashed potato soup:

Ingredients: Leftover mashed potatoes, vegetable puree, and canned broth from Day 1; 1 tsp. salt; 1 tsp. pepper; milk (if needed); ½ jar bacon pieces; 1 cup shredded cheddar cheese.

Directions: In a soup pot, combine all ingredients except bacon bits, milk, and cheese. Add milk if the soup is too thick. Heat through. Top the individual servings with bacon bits and cheese.

Day 3

Cincinnati chili spaghetti:

Ingredients: 2 lbs. ground beef; 2 onions, chopped; 1 tsp. allspice, 1 tsp. cinnamon; 1 tsp. garlic powder; 1 tsp. cayenne or red pepper flakes; 2-3 Tbsp. chili powder; 1 tsp. ground cumin; 1 Tbsp. red wine vinegar; 4 bay leaves; 1 tsp. salt; 1 tsp. pepper; 15 oz. tomato sauce; 15 oz. can diced tomatoes with green chilies; 2 cups water; shredded cheddar cheese; extra chopped onion; cooked spaghetti noodles.

Directions: Brown ground beef and onion together; drain and transfer to a large pot. Add remaining ingredients. Bring to a boil. Reduce heat and simmer for 3 hours. Remove bay leaves. Cook spaghetti according to package directions. Serve chili over hot spaghetti. Top with shredded cheese and extra chopped onion.
*Note: I usually put this together in my crock pot the night before and cook it on low while I'm at work the next day.

Dark green salad:

Ingredients: 1 bag fresh baby spinach leaves; 4 or 5 green onions, sliced; 1 cucumber, peeled and sliced; 2 stalks celery, sliced.

Directions: Toss all ingredients together in a large bowl.

Garden herb vinaigrette:

Ingredients: 1 Tbsp. fresh basil, 1 Tbsp. fresh parsley; ½ Tbsp. fresh oregano; ⅔ cup olive oil; ⅓ cup red wine vinegar; 1 garlic clove, minced; ½ tsp. salt; ½ tsp. ground mustard.
Note: if you have an herb garden, use it!

Directions: Chop and measure herbs. Combine all ingredients in a jar with a tight fitting lid (like a canning jar). Shake vigorously. Drizzle ¼ cup dressing lightly over salad and toss gently.

Day 4

Bean burritos:

Ingredients: 2 cans refried beans; 1 cup salsa; flour tortillas; shredded cheddar cheese; sour cream.

Directions: In a microwave-safe bowl, combine beans and salsa. Microwave mixture on full power for about 3 minutes. Stir well. For each burrito, spread about ¼ cup beans into a flour tortilla, top with cheese and sour cream, tuck one end up and roll.

Tortilla chips and chili dip:

Ingredients: 2 packages cream cheese, softened; 2 cups leftover Cincinnati chili; 1 cup shredded cheddar cheese; tortilla chips.

Directions: Spray a pie plate with cooking oil. Press softened cream into pie plate. Top with chili. Bake in a 350 degree oven for 10 minutes. Remove from oven and top with cheese. Serve with tortillas.

Day 5

Grilled steaks:

Ingredients: Steaks; steak seasoning; Worcestershire sauce.

Directions: Sprinkle steaks with Worcestershire sauce and steak seasoning. Marinate 1 hour or more. Grill to desired doneness (use a meat thermometer if you need to).

Broccoli, rice, and bean salad:

Ingredients: 1 lb broccoli, cut into florets; 1 15 oz. can kidney beans, rinsed and drained; ½ cup sliced celery; ¼ cup diced red onion; ½ jar bacon bits; 1 cup cooked brown rice; leftover garden vinaigrette from Day 3.

Directions: Cook rice according to package directions; place in a large bowl and put it in the refrigerator to chill. Blanch broccoli in boiling water 1 minute; rinse with cold water and drain; add to rice. Add beans, celery, bacon bits, and onion to rice. Top with ½ - ¾ cups garden herb vinaigrette and mix well. Chill for 2 hours.

Day 6

French onion soup:

Ingredients: 3 lbs. onions, skins removed, cut in half, and sliced; 2 garlic cloves, minced; 1 stick butter; 1 Tbsp. balsamic vinegar; 2 tsp. Worcestershire sauce; 1 tsp. black pepper; 6 cans beef broth (I usually use low sodium); 1 ½ cups shredded mozzarella cheese; ¼ cup grated Parmesan cheese; croutons.

Directions: Melt butter in a large pot. Add onions and garlic. Stir, cover, and cook for about 5 minutes. Remove cover, stir, cover, and cook for another 5 minutes. Repeat this process until the onions are limp and beginning to brown. Stir in vinegar, Worcestershire sauce, and black pepper. Add broth and bring to a boil. Reduce heat, cover, and cook for another 30 minutes. To serve, ladle the soup into bowls, top with croutons, grated Parmesan cheese, and shredded mozzarella.

Reuben Sandwiches

Ingredients: *Per person*: 2 slices rye bread; ¼ lb. thinly sliced deli corned beef; 1 slice Swiss cheese; ¼ cup sauerkraut; 1 Tbsp. Thousand Island dressing.

Directions: Preheat a Foreman grill (or a pancake griddle). Drain sauerkraut and heat on the grill for 3-5 minutes; remove and set aside. Place corned beef on the grill and heat for 3-5 minutes; remove and set aside. Place ½ of the rye bread on the grill. Layer the bread with sauerkraut, meat, and cheese. Top with remaining rye bread slices that have been spread with Thousand Island dressing. Close grill and cook for about 2 minutes. Remove, cut in half, and serve.

Day 7

Lori's quiches:

Ingredients: 1 lb. sausage or bacon, cooked, drained, and crumbled; 1 cup baking mix; 8 eggs; 2 ½ cups milk; ½ tsp. salt; ½ tsp. pepper; 1 cup shredded cheddar cheese.

Directions: Combine all ingredients. Pour into 2 greased pie plates. Bake at 375 degrees for 35-40 minutes.

Mixed fresh fruit:

Ingredients: 4 cups fresh fruit of your choice. Bananas, melon, strawberries, blueberries, etc; strawberry yogurt.

Directions: Cut fruit into bite-sized pieces. Top with yogurt. Stir gently and serve.

Week 9

57.   Hamburgers
       a.   Sour cream and chive potato casserole
       b.   Fried green tomatoes

58.   Feta chicken
       a.   Mediterranean vegetables

59.   Baked spaghetti
       a.   Salad
       b.   Garlic bread

60.   Mexi-meatloaf
       a.   Spicy rice

61.   No peek beef
       a.   Egg noodles
       b.   Peas

62.   Chicken and broccoli casserole
       a.   Baked potatoes

63.   Bean soup
       a.   Corn bread

Shopping List for Week 9

Ground beef (½ lb. 1½ lb. 2 lb.)
1 pkg. wheat sandwich buns
1 bag frozen shredded hash browns
16 oz. cheddar cheese
1 jar real mayonnaise
Bread crumbs
Fresh parsley
1 bunch green onions
8 oz. fresh mushrooms
8 oz. snow peas
8 oz. feta cheese
8 oz. cherry tomatoes
1 lb. wheat spaghetti noodles
2 bags frozen broccoli
1 jar green olives
1 bag chili-cheese Fritos
1 envelope taco seasoning
2 pkgs. frozen egg noodles
1 loaf Italian bread
1 envelope dry onion soup mix
1 dozen eggs
1 lb. dry Northern beans
1 4 oz. can black olives
Grated Parmesan cheese
2 (16 oz.) bags frozen broccoli

Corn meal
16 oz. cottage cheese
16 oz. sour cream
2 large green tomatoes
Cooking Sherry
12 boneless chicken breasts
Fresh basil
2 cucumbers
8 oz. mozzarella
1 lb. carrots
½ lb. asparagus
1 Yellow bell pepper
1 (10 oz.) pkg. frozen peas

1 red onion
1 (10 oz.) pkg. frozen corn
1 lb. brown rice
Salad greens
5 lbs. potatoes
2 (16 oz.) cans green beans
1 lb. Italian sausage
2 ham hocks
1 bunch broccoli
16 oz. stewed tomatoes
28 oz. diced tomatoes

15 oz. can diced tomatoes with green chiles
1 family size can cream of mushroom soup

1 8 oz. can marinated artichoke hearts
4 (10 ½ oz.) cans cream of chicken soup
1 jar spaghetti sauce (store bought or Angie's recipe)
Taco sauce (store bought or Angie's recipe)
3-4 lbs. beef stew meat or a roast cut up

Recipes for Week 9

Day 1

Hamburgers:

Ingredients: 1 ½ lbs. ground chuck; 1 Tbsp. steak seasoning; 2 Tbsp. ketchup; 1 Tbsp. Worcestershire sauce; wheat hamburger buns; lettuce; tomato; sliced red onion; and your favorite condiments.

Directions: In a large bowl, thoroughly mix meat, steak seasoning, ketchup, and Worcestershire sauce. Shape into patties. Either grill outside on a gas or charcoal grill or indoors on a George Foreman grill until burgers are well done. Serve on wheat hamburger buns with lettuce, tomato, onions, and condiments of your choice.

Sour cream and chive potato casserole:

Ingredients: 1 package frozen shredded hash browns, thawed; 1 small onion, diced; 8 oz. sour cream; 1 can cream of chicken soup; 1 stick butter, melted; 1 cup cheddar cheese, shredded; ½ cup fresh(or frozen) garlic chives, minced.

Directions: In a large bowl, combine all ingredients. Transfer to a large greased casserole dish. Cover and bake at 350 degrees for 30 minutes. Remove cover and bake 15 minutes longer.

Fried green tomatoes:

Ingredients: 3 large fresh green tomatoes; ¾ cup oil; 1 egg plus ¼ cup water; ½ cup corn meal; ¼ cup wheat flour; 1 Tbsp. Cajun seasoning; salt to taste.

Directions: Heat oil in a skillet. Wash and slice tomatoes. Whisk egg and water together in a shallow bowl. Mix corn meal, wheat flour, and Cajun seasoning in another shallow bowl. Dip tomato slices in egg wash and then dredge though corn meal mixture. Fry tomatoes for 2-3 minutes on each side and drain on paper towels. Salt the tomatoes before serving.

Day 2

Feta Chicken:

Ingredients: Marinade: ⅔ cup olive oil; ⅔ cup red wine vinegar; ½ cup chopped fresh parsley; 4 cloves garlic, crushed; 2 Tbsp. Dijon mustard2 tsp. sugar; 2 Tbsp. fresh basil; ½ tsp. salt; ½ tsp. pepper. 6-8 boneless, skinless chicken breasts; 1 can stewed tomatoes; 1 small can sliced olives; 1 tsp. oregano; 2 tsp. basil; ¼ cup crumbled feta cheese.

Directions: Combine ingredients for marinade in a blender; you will use half for the chicken and the other half for the salad. ***Do not use any of the marinade that has come into contact with the chicken in the salad!*** Place chicken in a large glass dish or a sealable plastic bag and pour ½ the marinade over chicken. Turn chicken to coat. Marinate 1 hour or longer. Grill chicken 5-7 minutes per side. Remove from grill onto a serving dish; sprinkle with oregano and basil and cover with foil for 5-10 minutes. Meanwhile, drain stewed tomatoes and olives; heat together in a small saucepan. Top each grilled chicken breast with a little bit of the tomato and olive mixture and crumbled feta cheese.

Mediterranean vegetables:

Ingredients: *Unused* marinade from chicken recipe; ¼ cup feta cheese (crumbled); 4-6 cups assorted vegetables: broccoli; carrots; celery; green onion; yellow pepper; asparagus; marinated artichoke hearts (drained and chopped); cherry tomatoes; snow peas; mushrooms.

Directions: Wash and chop veggies. Place in a large salad bowl. Stir cheese into marinade and pour over veggies. Toss well. Cover and chill for at least 2 hours.

Day 3

Baked spaghetti:

Ingredients: 1 lb. ground beef; 1 lb. Italian sausage; 2 cloves garlic, minced; 2 onions, chopped; 2 Tbsp. fresh parsley, divided; 2 tsp. basil, 1 tsp. oregano; 1 tsp. thyme; 1 tsp. pepper; 1 tsp. salt; 1 lb. spaghetti noodles; 2 cups cottage cheese; ¼ cup Parmesan cheese; 1 egg; 8 oz. mozzarella, shredded; 1 jar spaghetti sauce, 1 large can diced tomatoes (undrained).

Directions: Brown ground beef, sausage, garlic, and onion together; drain and transfer to a large pot. Add 1 Tbsp. fresh parsley, 2 tsp. basil, 1 tsp. oregano, 1 tsp. thyme, 1 tsp. pepper, 1 tsp. salt, 1 jar spaghetti sauce, and large can diced tomatoes (undrained). Bring to a boil and simmer for 30 minutes. Meanwhile, cook spaghetti noodles according to package directions and drain. Spray a lasagna pan with cooking spray and spread about a cup of sauce around the bottom of the pan. Place ½ of the noodles in the pan and spread toward the sides. In a medium bowl, mix cottage cheese, Parmesan cheese, 1 Tbsp. parsley, and egg. Spread cottage cheese mixture over the noodles in the pan and top with remaining noodles. Pour sauce over noodles to cover. Be sure to get the sauce all the way into the corners. Top with shredded mozzarella cheese. Cover with foil. Bake at 350 degrees for 45 minutes; remove foil and bake 15 minutes longer.

*Note: I usually put this together the night before and cook it the next day; just increase the cooking time by about 30 minutes.

Salad:

Ingredients: Salad greens; carrots; celery; cucumber.

Directions: Tear salad greens into bite-sized pieces and chop carrots, celery, and cucumber. Toss all ingredients together in a large bowl. Top with your favorite Italian dressing.

*Note: if you have any leftover Mediterranean salad, use that instead of the carrots, celery, and cucumber and just toss it with the salad greens.

Garlic bread:

Ingredients: 1 loaf Italian bread, split lengthwise; 2 cloves garlic, minced; 2 tsp. parsley; 1 stick butter, softened.

Directions: Place bread halves on a cookie sheet. Mix garlic, butter, and parsley with a hand mixer until it's creamy. Spread butter mixture over bread. Bake uncovered for 10-15 minutes at 350 degrees.

Day 4

Mexi-meatloaf:

Ingredients: 1 ½ lbs. ground beef; red onion, chopped; 2 Tbsp. green olives, chopped; 1 cup frozen corn; 1 envelope taco seasoning; 1 cup taco sauce, divided; 1 ½ cups crushed chili cheese Fritos; 1 egg; 1 tsp. pepper; 2 tsp. chili powder.

Directions: In large mixing bowl, combine ½ cup of taco sauce with the remaining ingredients. Shape into a loaf and bake for 45 minutes at 350 degrees. Top with remaining taco sauce and bake 15 minutes longer.

Spicy rice:

Ingredients: 2 cups brown rice; 4 cups water; 2 tsp. butter; 1 onion, chopped; 1 garlic clove chopped; 1 can diced tomatoes with green chilies; 2-4 tsp. chili powder; 1 tsp. ground cumin.

Directions: Melt butter, sauté onion and garlic. Add rice, water, undrained diced tomatoes, and seasonings. Cook according to package directions. Fluff with a fork before serving.

Day 5

No-peek beef:

Ingredients: 3 lbs. beef stew meat (or a roast cut into bite-sized portions); 1 large can cream of mushroom soup; 1 envelope dry onion soup mix; 1 tsp. pepper.

Directions: Mix all ingredients together in a large covered casserole. Cover with lid. Bake at 350 degrees for 3 hours. Don't peek! Serve over egg noodles.

Egg noodles:

Ingredients: 2 packages frozen egg noodles

Directions: Cook noodles according to package directions.

Peas:

Ingredients: 1 package frozen peas; butter.

Directions: Cook according to package directions and top with a pat of butter; stir.

Day 6

Chicken and broccoli casserole:

Ingredients: 2 frozen bags broccoli; 6 chicken breasts; 3 cans cream of chicken soup; 1 ½ cup real mayonnaise; 2 tsp. lemon juice; ¼ cup sherry; 8 oz. cheddar cheese, shredded; ¾ cup soft bread crumbs; 2 Tbsp. melted butter.

Directions: Boil chicken until done; cool and cut into bite-sized pieces. In a large bowl, mix cream of chicken soup, lemon juice, and sherry. In a greased, large rectangular casserole dish arrange ingredients in the following order: broccoli, chicken, chicken soup mix, cheese, and bread crumbs. Drizzle butter over bread crumbs and cover with foil. Bake at 350 degrees for 1 hour (it will be bubbly and hot!) Uncover during the last 15 minutes of baking.

Baked potatoes:

Ingredients: 6 potatoes, cooking oil spray.

Directions: Scrub potatoes; pierce with a fork. Place in a glass pie plate. Spray with cooking oil spray and cover with foil. Bake at 350 degrees for 1 hour.
* Note: you can serve the potatoes with butter and sour cream OR you can spoon the chicken broccoli casserole over them.

Day 7

Bean soup:

Ingredients: 1 lb. dry white beans, soaked overnight and rinsed; 2 smoked ham hocks; 3 quarts water; 3 onions, diced; 4 stalks celery, sliced; 2 carrots, peeled and sliced; 1 Tbsp. parsley; ½ cup instant mashed potato flakes; 2 tsp. salt; 1 tsp. pepper.
Directions: Combine all ingredients except mashed potato flakes in a crock pot. Cook on low 8hours. Take out ham hocks and remove meat from bones. Diced meat and return to crock pot; discard bones and fat. Add mashed potato flakes and cook 1 hour longer.

Corn bread:

Ingredients: 1 cup cornmeal; 1 cup flour;   cup sugar; 2 tsp. baking powder; ½ tsp. salt; 1 egg, beaten; ¼ cup oil **or** melted butter; 1 cup milk **or** buttermilk.

Directions: In a large bowl, mix together the dry ingredients. Add egg, oil, and milk, stir gently to combine. Spoon the batter into a greased oven-safe skillet or pie pan. Bake at 400 degrees for 15-20 minutes.

Week 10

64. Chicken rosemary
   a. Wild rice casserole
   b. Spinach salad

65. Breakfast sandwiches
   a. Hash browns

66. Smoked sausage
   a. Stovetop macaroni
   b. Bacon coleslaw

67. Tacos
   a. Spicy bean salad

68. Baked ham
   a. Sweet potato casserole
   b. Greens

69. Ham balls (uses leftover ham from Day 5)
   a. 7 layer salad

70. Hot Italian subs
   a. Veggies and dip

Shopping List for Week 10

6 boneless chicken breasts
Grated Parmesan cheese
1 lb. brown rice
1 lb. fresh mushrooms
1 bag fresh baby spinach leaves
1 Red onion
2 lbs. bulk sausage
10 frozen hash brown patties
1 sm. can peanuts
24 oz. cheddar cheese
2 lbs. ground beef
1 head iceberg lettuce
1 small red cabbage
15 oz. can black beans
15 oz. can garbanzo beans
3-4 lb. boneless ham
2 (32 oz.) sweet potatoes in water
2 cups chopped pecans
10 oz. frozen collard greens
10 oz. frozen peas
1 pkg. (8-10) Sub buns
½ lb. deli turkey
½ lb. sandwich-sized deli pepperoni
1 jar banana pepper rings
Miracle Whip
16 oz. sour cream
½ cup slivered almonds
2 lbs. smoked sausage
3 lbs. onions
Salsa (store-bought or Angie's recipe)

1 jar Dijon mustard
8 oz. wild rice
1 quart chicken broth
½ lb. cherry tomatoes
1 lb. bacon
Catalina salad dressing
6 English muffins
1 dozen eggs
1 lb. macaroni noodles
Milk
Taco shells (hard or soft)
1 med. green cabbage
16 oz. can kidney beans
10 oz. bag frozen corn
Lime juice
1 lb. ground pork
1 envelope taco seasoning
16 oz. pizza sauce
1 bunch celery
1 green pepper
1 lb. deli ham
¼ lb. deli Colby cheese
¼ lb. provolone slices
1 bag potato chips
1 garlic bulb
1 lb. brown sugar
Fresh garlic chives
1 can spicy V-8 juice

Recipes for Week 10

Day 1

Chicken rosemary:

Ingredients: 6 boneless chicken breasts; 6 Tbsp. Dijon mustard; 1 tsp. garlic powder; 1 Tbsp. dried rosemary, crushed; 1 tsp. pepper; Parmesan cheese.

Directions: Place chicken in a greased baking dish. Combine mustard, garlic powder, and pepper; spread over chicken. Sprinkle with rosemary and parmesan cheese. Bake, uncovered at 350 degrees for 45 minutes or until juices run clear.

Wild rice casserole:

Ingredients: ½ cup wild rice; 3/4 cup brown rice; ¼ cup oil; ½ cup slivered almonds; 1 Tbsp. garlic chives; 2 cups fresh mushrooms, sliced; 1 onion, diced; 1 garlic clove, minced; 1 quart chicken broth.

Directions: Add rice, oil, nuts, chives, mushrooms, onion, garlic chives, and garlic together in a skillet. Cook and stir 20 minutes. Heat the broth to boiling. Pour all into a greased 2 quart casserole. Cover and bake at 350 degrees for 1 ½ hours or until liquid is absorbed and rice is fluffy.

Spinach salad:

Ingredients: 1 bag fresh spinach; ½ cup cherry tomatoes, cut in half; ½ lb. bacon, diced; ⅓ cup Catalina salad dressing; ½ tsp. prepared mustard; ¼ tsp. salt; ¼ tsp. pepper; 1 cup fresh mushrooms, sliced; 2 hard cooked eggs, sliced; ½ red onion, sliced.

Directions: In a skillet, cook bacon until crisp, remove to paper towels and set aside. Drain skillet, reserving 2 Tbsp. bacon drippings. Add the salad dressing, mustard, salt, and pepper. Cook and stir over low heat until heated through. In a large salad bowl, combine spinach, red onion, cherry tomatoes, mushroom, bacon, and egg. Drizzle with warm dressing and toss gently to coat.

Day 2

Breakfast sandwiches:

Ingredients: 2 lbs. bulk sausage; 6 cheese slices; 1 Tbsp. butter; 6 eggs; salt and pepper; 6 English muffins, toasted.

Directions: Shape sausage into 6 patties, fry in a skillet or grill on a Foreman grill; remove to paper towels when done. Meanwhile, melt butter in a large skillet. Carefully break each egg into the butter and break each yolk with a fork; salt and pepper to taste. Carefully turn eggs after a minute or two. Cook for another minute or two, or until desired doneness. For each sandwich, place a slice of cheese, an egg, and a sausage patty in an English muffin.

Hash brown patties:

Ingredients: Frozen hash brown patties; cooking spray.

Directions: Spray a baking sheet or baking stone with cooking spray. Place hash brown patties on the sheet or stone and spray again. Bake according to package directions.

Day 3

Smoked sausage:

Ingredients: 2 lbs smoked sausage, cut into 4-6 inch pieces and split lengthwise.

Directions: Grill sausage on a Foreman grill or fry in a skillet until browned and heated through.

Stovetop macaroni:

Ingredients: 2 cups macaroni noodles, 1 Tbsp. butter; 1 Tbsp. flour; 1 tsp. salt; ½ tsp. pepper; 8 oz. cheddar cheese, shredded; approximately 1 cup milk.

Directions: Cook macaroni according to package directions, drain and set aside, toss with a little butter to prevent sticking. Meanwhile, in a large saucepan, melt butter. Add flour, salt, and pepper to melted butter, cook and stir for about 2 minutes. Gradually add 1 cup milk (more or less as needed) until a creamy white sauce is created. Add shredded cheese, stirring until melted. Add noodles and serve.

Bacon coleslaw:

Ingredients: ¾ cup Miracle whip; 1 Tbsp. sugar; 1 ½ tsp. red wine vinegar; 4 cups shredded green cabbage (about 1 medium head); 1

cup shredded red cabbage (about ½ small head); ½ cup chopped peanuts; ½ lb. bacon.

Directions: Cook bacon until done, remove to paper towels and dice. Reserve 2 Tbsp. of the bacon drippings for Day 5 and place in a container in the refrigerator. Mix the Miracle Whip, sugar, and vinegar in a large bowl. Add remaining ingredients; mix until cabbage is coated with dressing. Refrigerate until serving.

Day 4

Tacos:

Ingredients: 2 lbs. ground beef; 1 large onion, diced; 1 envelope taco seasoning; 1 Tbsp. chili powder; 1 tsp. ground cumin; 1 can Spicy V-8 juice; 1 can diced tomatoes with green chilies; lettuce, shredded cheddar cheese; sour cream; salsa; and taco shells.

Directions: Brown ground beef and diced onions; drain. Add remaining ingredients. Simmer for about 30 minutes. Serve in taco shells with lettuce, salsa, shredded cheese, and sour cream.

Spicy bean salad:

Ingredients: 1 can kidney beans, 1 can black beans, 1 can garbanzo beans; 2 celery ribs, sliced; ½ of a red onion, diced; 1 cup frozen corn, thawed; ¾ cup salsa; 2 Tbsp. oil; ¼ cup lime juice; 2 tsp. chili powder; 1 tsp. salt; 1 tsp. ground cumin.

Directions: In a bowl, combine beans, celery, onion, and corn. In a small bowl, combine salsa, oil, lime juice, chili powder, salt, and cumin; mix well. Pour over the bean mixture and toss to coat. Cover and refrigerate until serving.

Day 5

Baked ham:

Ingredients: 1 medium boneless ham, ½ cup brown sugar.

Directions: Rinse ham and rub with brown sugar. Place in a heavy pan and cover with foil. Bake at 350 degrees for about 3 hours. Allow to stand for 15 minutes before slicing. Slice with an electric knife.

Sweet potato casserole:

Ingredients: 2 large cans sweet potatoes in water, drained; 2 cups sugar; 1 tsp. salt; 4 eggs; ½ cup milk; 2 sticks butter (softened and divided); dash cinnamon; 2 tsp. vanilla extract; 2 cups brown sugar; 2 cups chopped pecans; 1 cup flour.

Directions: In a large bowl, mix sweet potatoes, sugar, salt, eggs, 1 stick softened butter, cinnamon, and vanilla with a hand mixer. Pour into a greased 9x13 inch pan. Melt the other stick of butter in a saucepan. In another large bowl, mix brown sugar, chopped pecans, flour, and melted butter until crumbly. Spread over potatoes. Bake the casserole, uncovered, at 350 degrees for 40-50 minutes.

Greens:

Ingredients: 1 package frozen greens, thawed; 1 small onion, diced; reserved bacon drippings from Day 3.

Directions: Melt bacon dripping in a saucepan. Sauté the onion in the drippings. Add thawed greens and heat through.

Day 6

Ham balls:

Ingredients: 1 lb. ground pork; 1 lb. leftover ham from Day 5, chopped finely in a food processor; 2 eggs; ¾ cup milk; ⅔ cup dry bread crumbs; 1 ½ cups brown sugar; ⅔ cup water (or pineapple juice if you happen to have some!); ⅓ cup vinegar; ¾ tsp. ground mustard.

Directions: In a bowl, combine the pork, ham, eggs, milk, and bread crumbs; mix well. Shape into 1 ½ to 2 inch balls; place in a greased baking dish. In a saucepan, combine brown sugar, water (or juice), vinegar, and mustard. Bring to a boil over medium heat. Reduce heat and simmer, uncovered, for 4 minutes. Pour over ham balls. Bake, uncovered, at 350 degrees for 60-70 minutes or until browned.

7 layer salad:

Ingredients: ½ head lettuce, torn; ½ cup sliced celery; 1 green pepper, diced; 1 package frozen peas, thawed; 1 onion, diced; ½ cup cherry tomatoes, chopped; ¾ cup miracle whip; 2 Tbsp. oil; 2 Tbsp. sugar; ¼ cup Parmesan cheese; 1 cup shredded cheddar cheese.

Directions: In a large bowl, layer the vegetables in the following order: lettuce, celery, pepper, peas, onion, and tomato. Mix together Miracle Whip, oil, sugar, and parmesan cheese. Spread evenly over vegetables. Top with shredded cheese. Chill for several hours or overnight.

Day 7

Hot Italian subs:

Ingredients: 1 lb. deli ham; ½ lb. deli turkey; ½ lb. deli sandwich pepperoni; red onion, sliced; pickled banana pepper slices; ¼ lb. sliced Colby cheese; ¼ lb. sliced provolone cheese; pizza sauce; sub buns.

Directions: For each sandwich, spread pizza sauce on the inside of the bottom and top sub bun. Layer the ham, pepperoni, provolone, turkey, banana peppers, red onion, and provolone cheese on the sub bun. Bake at 350 degrees for 10 minutes. Serve with your family's favorite potato chips.

Week 11

71. Chicken Parmesan
    a. Pasta salad

72. Roast with veggies (crock-pot recipe)
    a. Beer biscuits

73. Bandits (uses leftover roast from Day 2)
    a. Tortilla chips and salsa

74. Sloppy Joes
    a. Sweet potato fries
    b. Broccoli salad

75. Garlic lime chicken
    a. Hint of lime potato wedges
    b. California blend veggies

76. Mandarin chicken salad (uses leftover chicken from Day 5)

77. Cheesy ham and potatoes
    a. Asparagus and leeks

Shopping List for Week 11

18 boneless chicken breasts
Grated Parmesan cheese
2 bunches green onion
2 lbs. carrots
6 oz. can black olives
2 bunches broccoli
10 lbs. potatoes
8-10 burrito-sized flour tortillas
16 oz. kidney beans
4 large sweet potatoes
1 ½ lbs. ground beef
1 jar fully cooked bacon bits
4 oz. shelled sunflower seeds
1 garlic bulb
1 envelope taco seasoning
2 heads lettuce
Taco seasoning
1 cup cashews
1 lb. asparagus spears
8 oz. snow peas
8 oz. mozzarella
1 envelope dry onion soup mix
1 (10 ½ oz.) can beef broth
1 bag frozen diced hash browns
1 (15 oz.) can tomato sauce
Salsa (store-bought or Angie's recipe)
Toasted sesame (or other Asian type) salad dressing
1 (15 oz.) can mandarin orange segments
15 oz. diced tomatoes with green chiles
1 bag (16 oz.) frozen California blend vegetables

28 oz. spaghetti sauce
1 lb. spiral pasta
2 tomatoes
Italian salad dressing
8 oz. mushrooms
4-5 lb. roast
3 lbs. onions
16 oz. cheddar cheese
1 pkg. hamburger buns
1 red onion
1 Cucumber
1 small head cauliflower
Lime juice
1 lb. bacon
1 bottle of beer
15 oz. can tomato sauce
Chow mein noodles
1 lb. cubed ham
6 leeks
8 oz. bean sprouts
16 oz. sour cream
1 green pepper
24 oz. refried beans
8 oz. pepper jack cheese
1 bag tortilla chips

Recipes for Week 11

Day 1

Chicken Parmesan:

Ingredients: 6 boneless chicken breasts; ¾ cup seasoned dry bread crumbs; ¾ cup Parmesan cheese; 1 tsp. oregano; 1 tsp. basil; 1 tsp. garlic powder; 1 cup shredded mozzarella; 2 Tbsp. oil; 28 oz. spaghetti sauce.

Directions: Heat oil in a large skillet. Mix bread crumbs, Parmesan cheese, and seasonings. Dredge chicken through bread crumb mixture and brown on each side in oil. Transfer to a greased baking dish and top each chicken breast with about a ½ cup spaghetti sauce. Bake, uncovered at 350 degrees for 45 minutes or until juices run clear. Top each chicken breast with mozzarella cheese shreds during the last 5 minutes of baking.

Pasta salad:

Ingredients: 1 box spiral pasta; 1 cucumber, peeled, seeded, and chopped; 3 green onions, sliced; 1 small can black olives, drained; 2 carrots, peeled and thinly sliced; 1 tomato, seeded and chopped; ½ bar mozzarella, cubed; 1 green pepper, diced; 1 cup mushrooms, sliced; 1 cup Italian salad dressing.

Directions: Cook pasta according to package directions, drain and rinse with cold water. Place in a salad bowl and add remaining ingredients; toss well and chill.

113

Day 2

Roast with veggies:

Ingredients: 4-5lb. roast; 6 carrots, peeled; 3 onions, peeled and quartered; 6 potatoes, peeled; 1 envelope dry onion soup mix; 1 (10 ½ oz.) can beef broth.
Directions: Rinse roast; place in crock pot and pat all over with onion soup. Add veggies to the pot and pour beef broth over all. Cook on low 8-10 hours.

Beer biscuits:

Ingredients: 2 cups Bisquick; 2 Tbsp. sugar; 8 oz. room temperature beer.

Directions: Mix ingredients until just combined. Bake at 450 degrees in well greased muffin pans until done (8-10 minutes).

Day 3

Bandits:

Ingredients: Leftover roast, shredded; 1 can diced tomatoes with green chiles; 1 envelope taco seasoning mix; 1 large can refried beans; ½ cup salsa; burrito-sized flour tortillas; ¼ cup oil; 8 oz. shredded cheddar cheese; 2 cups shredded lettuce; 1 tomato, diced; sour cream.
Directions: Combine beef, diced tomatoes with green chiles, and taco seasoning in a saucepan and heat through. Meanwhile, heat ¼ cup oil in a frying pan. In the center of each flour tortilla, spoon about ½ cup of the shredded meat. Fold into a square by bringing the sides

into the center and folding over twice; secure with a toothpick; now you have a "Bandit." Brown bandit in oil on both sides; drain on paper towels. Mix salsa and refried beans; heat for 3 minutes in the microwave. Top each bandit with about ½ cup refried beans, lettuce, tomato, cheese, and sour cream. Serve with tortilla chips and salsa.

Day 4

Sloppy Joes:

Ingredients: 1 ½ lbs. ground beef; 1 onion, diced; ⅓ cup ketchup; 2 Tbsp brown sugar; 2 Tbsp. vinegar; 2 tsp. Worcestershire sauce; hamburger buns.

Directions: Brown ground beef and diced onions; drain. Add remaining ingredients. Simmer for about 30 minutes. Serve on hamburger buns.

Sweet potato fries:

Ingredients: 4 sweet potatoes; 3-4 Tbsp. olive oil; 2 tsp. salt; 2-3 tsp. chili powder.

Directions: Scrub potatoes and cut into sticks. In a large bowl, toss potato sticks with oil, salt, and chili powder. Spread potatoes on a greased baking sheet and bake at 425 degrees for 20 minutes, turning once.

Broccoli salad:

Ingredients: 2 bunches broccoli, cut into florets; 1 small head cauliflower, cut into florets; 1 red onion, diced; 1 jar fully cooked bacon pieces; 4 oz. shelled sunflower seeds; 1 cup Miracle Whip; ¼ cup red wine vinegar;   cup sugar.

Directions: Place the vegetables and sunflower seeds in a large bowl. Mix sugar, vinegar, and Miracle Whip in a medium bowl. Pour dressing over vegetables and toss to coat. Chill until serving.

Day 5

Garlic lime chicken:

Ingredients: 12 chicken breasts; 1 cup lime juice; ½ cup cider vinegar; 8 garlic cloves, minced; 3 tsp. oregano;1 Tbsp. coriander; 3 tsp. pepper; 2 tsp. salt; 2 tsp. paprika; ¼ cup oil.

Directions: Combine all ingredients except chicken and oil. Take 2 large resealable bags and place 6 chicken breasts and half the marinade in each. Seal bag and turn to coat; refrigerate overnight. Heat the oil in a large skillet. Discard marinade. Brown the chicken on both sides. Transfer chicken to a large baking dish. Bake, uncovered at 375 degrees 35 minutes or until juices run clear.
*Note: you will use your leftover chicken breasts for Day 6.

Hint of lime potato wedges:

Ingredients: ½ cup butter, melted; 1 Tbsp. lime juice; 1 tsp. dried thyme; 3 large potatoes (or 6 smaller ones); ¼ cup grated parmesan cheese; ½ tsp. salt; ½ tsp. paprika.

Directions: In a large bowl, combine the melted butter, lime juice, and thyme. Wash potatoes, but don't peel them. Cut each potato into 8 wedges (or 4 if you've used smaller potatoes); add to melted butter mixture and toss to coat. Place the potato wedges skin-side down on a greased baking sheet. Combine the parmesan cheese, salt, and paprika; sprinkle over the potatoes. Bake the potato wedges at 400 degrees for 30 minutes, or until the potatoes are tender.

California blend veggies:

Ingredients: 1 bag frozen California blend veggies (broccoli, cauliflower, and carrots); 1-2 tsp. dill weed; 1 tsp. salt; ½ Tbsp. butter.

Directions: Heat veggies per package directions; season with dill, salt, and butter; stir and serve.

Day 6

Mandarin chicken salad:

Ingredients: Leftover garlic lime chicken from Day 5, diced; 1 package fresh bean sprouts, rinsed and dried; 1 cup cashews, coarsely chopped; 1 (15oz.) can mandarin orange segments, drained; 1 ½ cups snow peas, cut in half; chow mien noodles; 1 head lettuce, torn into bite-sized pieces; sesame seed salad dressing.

Directions: Place lettuce, snow peas, and bean sprouts in a salad bowl; toss. For each serving, place a large handful of lettuce mixture on a plate and top with diced chicken, cashews, mandarin oranges, and chow mien noodles. Drizzle with salad dressing and serve.

Day 7

Cheesy Ham and potatoes:

Ingredients: 4 cups frozen hash brown potatoes, thawed; 1 cup shredded pepper jack cheese; 1 ½ cups diced ham; ¼ cup chopped green onions; 6 eggs, beaten; 1 (12 oz.) can evaporated milk; ½ tsp. salt; 1 tsp. pepper.

Directions: Preheat oven to 350 degrees. Grease a large baking dish. Arrange hash browns in the bottom of the baking dish. Sprinkle with cheese, ham, and green onions. In a medium bowl, mix the eggs and evaporated milk, pepper, and salt. Pour the egg mixture over everything in the pan. Bake for 50-60 minutes, or until a knife inserted in the middle comes out clean.

Asparagus and leeks:

Ingredients: 6 medium leeks; 1 lb. asparagus spears; 1 Tbsp. olive oil; ½ tsp. salt; ground pepper to taste.

Directions: Trim the roots off of the leeks. Then cut off the top where the dark green part starts. Cut in half lengthwise and soak in a bowl of cold water to loosen any dirt. Rinse well and pat dry with paper towels. Trim tough ends from asparagus (about 2 inches), rinse, and pat dry. Place leeks and asparagus in a roasting pan and drizzle with olive oil. Toss to coat, sprinkle with salt and pepper; toss again. Roast in a 350 degree oven for 25-30 minutes or until vegetables are fork tender.

Week 12

78. Meatball subs
    a. Veggies and dip

79. Pasta Fagioli (uses leftover meatballs from Day 1)
    a. Parmesan focaccia

80. Creamed chicken and noodles
    a. Mashed potatoes
    b. Peas

81. Hamburger pie (uses leftover potatoes from Day 3)
    a. Biscuits

82. Swiss steak
    a. Roasted potatoes
    b. Creamed corn

83. Grilled Teriyaki chicken
    a. Stir-fried vegetables
    b. Fried rice

84. Corn bread taco bake
    a. Southwestern roasted vegetables

Shopping List for Week 12

1 broiler-fryer chicken, cut up
6 boneless skinless chicken breasts
2 lbs. carrots
½ lb. fresh mushrooms
1 bottle (12 oz.) chili sauce
16 oz. sour cream
1 envelope dry ranch dressing mix
2 pkgs. frozen egg noodles
2 (10 ½ oz.) cans chicken broth
1 bunch celery
2 red bell peppers
2 (10 oz.) packages frozen corn
1 envelope taco seasoning
1 tube (10) Refrigerated biscuits
1 (16 oz.) can kidney beans
1 (10 ½ oz.) can tomato soup
1(28 oz.) jar spaghetti sauce
1 bunch broccoli
1 (6 oz.) can sliced water chestnuts
1 lb. brown rice
1 can (15 oz.) chili without meat
1 (16 oz.)can cannellini beans
1 lb. ditalini (or other small) pasta

Teriyaki sauce
Honey
10 lbs. potatoes
1 Garlic bulb
Ketchup
3 lbs. onions
2 lbs. red potatoes
1 tomato
1 green bell pepper
1 red onion
1 yellow squash
1 zucchini
1 yellow bell pepper
1 pkg. sub buns
1 (4 oz.) can tomato sauce
16 oz. cheddar cheese
1 package frozen peas
2 bunches green onion
8 oz. snow peas
2 lbs. round steak
1 can stewed tomatoes
1 can Mexican-style corn
8 oz. mozzarella slices

3 packages ground beef; (2) 1 ½ lb. and (1) 2 lb.
1 (10 oz.) package frozen creamed corn
1 family size can cream of chicken soup
2 packages (8.5 oz.) corn muffin mix
1 (16 oz.) can cut green beans

Recipes for Week 12

Day 1

Meatball subs:

Ingredients: 2 eggs; ⅓ cup milk; ½ cup finely chopped onion; 1 ½ tsp. salt; 2 lbs. ground beef; 2 garlic cloves, minced; 1 tsp. butter; 1 cup ketchup; ⅔ cup chili sauce; ¼ cup packed brown sugar; 2 Tbsp. Worcestershire sauce; 2 Tbsp. prepared mustard; ½ tsp. hot pepper sauce; 2 cups soft bread crumbs; ½ lb. mozzarella slices; sub buns.

Directions: In a bowl, beat eggs and milk. Stir in bread crumbs, chopped onion, and salt. Add beef; mix well. Shape into 1-inch balls. Place in a large-sided cookie sheet or baking dish. Bake, uncovered at 375 degrees for 20 minutes or until meat is no longer pink. Remove to a paper towel covered platter. In a large saucepan, sauté garlic in butter. Add ketchup, chili sauce, brown sugar, Worcestershire sauce; mustard, and hot pepper sauce. Bring to a boil; add meatballs. Reduce heat, cover and simmer for 30 minutes. For each sandwich: Spoon meatballs onto bottom sub bun, top with cheese slices and top bun.

Veggies and dip

Ingredients: Carrots; celery; 1 pint sour cream; 1 packet dry ranch dressing mix.

Directions: Peel and wash veggies. Cut carrots and celery into sticks. Mix sour cream and dry ranch dressing mix together with a fork.

Day 2

Pasta Fagioli:

Ingredients: Any leftover meatballs from Day 1; 3 Tbsp. olive oil; 1 onion, quartered, then halved; 2 cloves garlic, minced; 1 jar spaghetti sauce; 5 ½ cups water; 1 Tbsp. parsley; 1 ½ tsp. basil; 1 tsp. oregano; 2 tsp. beef bullion powder; 1 can cannellini beans, drained and rinsed; 1 can kidney beans, drained and rinsed; ⅓ cup parmesan cheese; 1 lb. ditalini pasta.

Directions: In a large pot over medium heat, sauté onion and garlic in olive oil. Reduce heat, stir in spaghetti sauce, meatballs, water, parsley, basil, oregano, bullion powder; cannellini beans, kidney beans, and Parmesan cheese (add more water if it's too thick). Simmer 1 hour. Meanwhile, cook pasta according to package directions and drain. Stir cooked pasta into soup and serve.

Parmesan focaccia:

Ingredients: 3 cups wheat bread flour; ¾ cup plus 3 Tbsp. water at 80 degrees; 3 Tbsp. butter, softened; 2 Tbsp. nonfat dry milk powder; 3 Tbsp. sugar; 1 ½ tsp. salt; 3 cups wheat bread flour; 2 ¼ tsp. active dry yeast; 2 Tbsp. olive oil; 4 Tbsp. Parmesan cheese; 1 tsp. garlic salt.

Directions: In your bread machine pan, place the first 7 ingredients in the order suggested by your bread machine manufacturer. Select the dough setting (check dough after 5 minutes of mixing; add 1 to 2 Tbsp. flour or water if needed). When the cycle is completed, turn dough onto a lightly floured surface. Cover and let rest for 15 minutes. Knead for 1 minute. Roll into a 15 inch by 10 inch rectangle. Transfer to a greased 15x10x1 inch baking pan. Press dough up the sides a bit. Cover and let rise 20-30 minutes. With a wooden spoon or your fingertips, make indentations at 1 inch intervals. Brush dough with olive oil; sprinkle with garlic salt and parmesan cheese. Bake at 400 degrees for 13-15 minutes or until lightly browned. Cool slightly. Cut into squares and serve warm.

Day 3

Creamed chicken and noodles:

Ingredients: 1 broiler-fryer chicken, cut up; 1 can chicken broth; 1 large can cream of chicken soup; 1 Tbsp. butter; 1 small onion, diced; 2 stalks celery, sliced thin; 2 packages frozen egg noodles.

Directions: Place chicken pieces in a large pot of salted water. Bring to a boil and cook for 20-30 minutes. Remove from water and cool; discard skin and pick chicken from the bone. Rinse the pot you boiled the chicken in to use again. Melt butter in the pot and sauté onion and celery. Add chicken broth, cream of chicken soup, and stir until smooth. Add chicken and heat through. Meanwhile, cook noodles according to package directions and drain. Add noodles to the chicken mixture and stir to combine.

Mashed potatoes

Ingredients: 5 lbs potatoes; salt and pepper to taste; 3/4 cup (or so) milk; 1 stick butter.

Directions: Add 2 tsp. salt to a large pot of water. Bring it to a boil. While the water is heating, wash and peel about 5 pounds of potatoes. You can leave the peel on half of them if you want more fiber and texture. Dice the potatoes and put them in the boiling water. Boil until fork-tender (20-30 minutes). Drain potatoes in a colander.

While the potatoes are draining, place a stick of butter in the bottom of the pot you cooked it in, if you are using a hand mixer, or in the bottom of the bowl of your standing mixer. Mash potatoes until large lumps are gone, add milk, salt, and pepper, and then mash until smooth.

Peas:

Ingredients: Frozen peas, butter, salt and pepper to taste.

Directions: Cook according to package directions and top with about 2 tsp. butter. Season to taste with salt and pepper; stir.

Day 4

Hamburger pie:

Ingredients: 1 ½ lbs. ground beef; 1 onion, diced; 1 (4 oz.) can tomato sauce; 1 tbsp. Worcestershire sauce; 1 can tomato soup; 1 can green beans, drained; 1 package frozen corn, cooked and drained; leftover mashed potatoes (about 2 cups); ½ tsp. salt; 1 tsp. pepper; ½ cup shredded cheddar cheese.

Directions: Brown ground beef and diced onions; drain. Place in a large casserole dish. Add remaining ingredients except potatoes and cheese. Stir to combine. Top with mashed potatoes. Bake at 350 degrees for 30 minutes. Top mashed potatoes with cheese and bake 5 minutes more.

Biscuits:

Ingredients: 1 can refrigerated biscuits.

Directions: Bake according to package directions.

Day 5

Swiss steak:

Ingredients: 2 lbs. round steak; ⅓ cup flour; 1 tsp. salt; ½ tsp. pepper; 2 Tbsp. oil; 1 can stewed tomatoes; 1 onion, diced; 2 garlic cloves, minced.

Directions: Cut steak into serving sizes. Combine flour, salt, and pepper; sprinkle over steak and pound into both sides. In a large skillet, over medium heat, brown steak on both sides in oil. Transfer to a greased baking dish. In a medium bowl, combine tomatoes, onion, and garlic; pour over steak. Cover and bake at 350 degrees for 1 ½-2 hours.

Herb roasted potatoes:

Ingredients: ½ cup whipped salad dressing; 1 Tbsp. each dried rosemary, garlic powder, and onion flakes; 1 tsp. seasoned salt; 1 Tbsp. water; 2 lbs unpeeled small red potatoes, washed and quartered.

Directions: Mix dressing, seasonings, and water in a large bowl. Add potatoes; toss to coat. Place potatoes on a large jellyroll pan that has been coated with cooking spray. Spray more cooking spray over the potatoes. Bake at 350 degrees for 45 minutes to an hour, stirring after 20 minutes.

*Note: If your family doesn't like rosemary, substitute dried oregano or basil.

Creamed corn:

Ingredients: 1 package frozen corn; 1 package frozen creamed corn.

Directions: Place the contents of both packages in a microwave-safe dish. Cook according to directions for 2 packages. Stir, salt and pepper to taste.

Day 6

Grilled Teriyaki Chicken:

Ingredients: ¾ cup Teriyaki sauce; 3 Tbsp. honey; 2 cloves garlic, minced; ½ tsp. vegetable oil; 6 boneless, skinless chicken.

Directions: Combine first 4 ingredients in a bowl; remove and reserve 3 Tbsp. of the mixture. Place the chicken in a large plastic food storage bag. Pour remaining Teriyaki mixture over the chicken. Press air out of bag; close the top securely. Turn over several times to coat chicken. Marinate 30 minutes or longer. Grill 5-6 minutes on each side, or until the chicken is no longer pink. Brush with reserved sauce during the last few minutes.

Stir-fried vegetables:

Ingredients: 1 green bell pepper, cut in strips; 1 red bell pepper, cut in strips; 2 carrots, cut into 2 inch sticks; 2 cups broccoli florets; 1 cup sugar snap peas, cut in half; 3 Tbsp. oil; 2 Tbsp. soy sauce; 1 tsp. ground ginger; 6 green onions, thinly sliced; 2 Tbsp. cornstarch; 1 can chicken broth.

Directions: In a large skillet or wok, sauté the peppers, carrots, and broccoli for 3-5 minutes. Combine soy sauce and ginger; add to pan; also add the onions to the pan. Cook and stir for 2 minutes. Combine cornstarch and broth until smooth; gradually stir into the vegetables. Cook and stir for 2-4 more minutes to thicken the sauce.

Fried rice:

Ingredients: 4 cups cooked brown rice; 1 onion, diced; 2 stalks celery, sliced; 1 clove garlic, minced; 1 carrot, sliced; 1 can sliced water chestnuts, drained; 1 Tbsp. oil; 2 eggs; 2 tsp. butter; 2 Tbsp. soy sauce.

Directions: Cook rice according to package directions; set aside. Melt butter in a small skillet, add eggs and scramble until done. Remove from skillet to a plate and chop into small pieces. In a large skillet, sauté onion, celery, garlic, carrots, and water chestnuts in oil for 3-5 minutes. Add rice, egg, and soy sauce. Heat through.

Day 7

Corn bread taco bake:

Ingredients: 1 ½ lbs. ground beef; 1 envelope taco seasoning; ½ cup water; 1 tsp. ground cumin; 1 can chili without meat; 8 oz. cheddar cheese, shredded; 2 packages corn muffin mix; 1 can Mexican-style corn, drained; 1 tomato, chopped; green onions, thinly sliced; sour cream and salsa (if desired.); 2 eggs and ⅔ cup milk.

Directions: Preheat oven to 375 degrees. In a large skillet, cook ground beef until no longer pink; drain. Add taco seasoning mix and water, cook and stir until thickened. Stir in chili and 1 cup of cheese. In a large bowl, prepare the corn muffin mixes, 2 eggs, and ⅔ cup milk. Stir in the Mexican-style corn and remaining cheese. Spoon the ground beef mixture into a large jellyroll pan (a cookie sheet with sides). Top with corn muffin mixture and spread it evenly to the edges of the pan. Bake for 15-20 minutes or until golden brown. Top with tomatoes, green onion, and, if desired, sour cream and salsa.

Southwestern roasted vegetables:

Ingredients: 1 red bell pepper, cut into large chunks; 1 yellow bell pepper, cut into large chunks; 1 yellow squash, cut into ½ inch pieces; 1 zucchini, cut into ½ inch pieces; ½ lb. whole fresh mushrooms; 3 Tbsp. oil; ½ tsp. ground cumin; 2 tsp. chili powder.

Directions: Place vegetables in a large, shallow baking dish; drizzle with oil and sprinkle with spices. Toss to coat. Bake at 375 degrees for 30 minutes.

Week 13

85. Chicken soup
     a.   Cheese Texas toast

86. Pigs in a blanket
     a.   Baked beans
     b.   Oven fries

87. Swiss chicken
     a.   Carrot and broccoli casserole

88. BBQ pork chops
     a.   Twice-baked potato casserole
     b.   Green beans

89. Layered ravioli casserole
     a.   Caesar salad

90. Sausage and egg casserole
     a.   Potato cakes

91. Beef stew (crock pot recipe)
     a.   Cheese scones

Shopping List for Week 13

2 bone-in chicken breasts
3 lbs. onions
2 lbs. carrots
8 oz. small pasta (like ditalini)
1 tube refrigerated crescent rolls
2 large cans baked beans
6 boneless skinless chicken breasts
Ritz crackers
6 lb. baby carrots
2 (10 ½ oz.) cans cheese soup
24 oz. mozzarella cheese
2 (15 oz.) can diced tomatoes
1 (15 oz.) can tomato puree
1 (15 oz.) can tomato sauce
2 (3 oz.) Italian tomato paste
Shredded Parmesan cheese
6-8 boneless pork loin chops
3 (8 oz.) cheddar cheese
1 jar fully cooked bacon pieces
2 tomatoes
2 (16 oz.) sour cream
1 box frozen cheese Texas toast

1 quart chicken broth
1 bunch celery
Brown rice
Grated Parmesan cheese
1 pkg. hot dogs
10 lbs.pPotatoes
1 lb. fresh mushrooms
6 slices ham
2 bunches fresh broccoli
2 pkgs. frozen ravioli
1 zucchini
1 bunch green onions
1 lb. Bacon
10 oz. pkg. frozen peas
3 hearts romaine lettuce
Croutons
2 (16 oz.) cans green beans
1 lb. sausage
Bisquick
1½ dozen eggs
1 pint buttermilk

3 lbs. beef stew meat (or a roast that you will cut up)
1 family size can cream of chicken soup
1 (10 ½ oz.) can beef broth

Recipes for Week 13

Day 1

Chicken Soup:

Ingredients: 2 bone-in chicken breasts; 1 quart chicken broth; 2 Tbsp. butter; 2 cups water; 3 carrots, peeled and sliced; 3 celery stalks, sliced; 1 large onion, diced; 2 cloves garlic; minced; ½ cup brown rice; 1 cup small pasta; 2 Tbsp. wild rice, if desired.

Directions: In a saucepan, cook chicken breasts in about a quart of water. Bring to a boil and then turn down to medium heat. Cook for 20-30 minutes. Remove from pan and place on a plate; discard cooking water. Put the plate of chicken in the refrigerator to cool. Melt butter in a large pot; add vegetables and sauté for about 5 minutes. Add broth, rice, and water; bring to a boil and then turn down to medium heat. Cook vegetables and rice for about half an hour. Meanwhile, remove skin from chicken and pull meat from the bones. Dice chicken and add to the pot. Add pasta and cook until chicken is heated through and pasta is tender (about 10-15 minutes).

Cheese Texas toast: 1 box frozen cheese Texas toast.

Directions: Prepare according to package directions.

Day 2

Pigs in a blanket:

Ingredients: 1 package hot dogs; 1 tube refrigerated crescent rolls; ketchup; 2 slices American cheese.

Directions: Open the tube of crescent rolls and separate the dough along the perforations. Cut a lengthwise slit in each hotdog. Place one hot dog on each piece of dough. Cut each slice of cheese into 4 strips. Stuff a cheese strip into each hot dog slit. Top the cheese with a thin line of ketchup. Fold dough around the hotdog and bake according to the crescent roll package directions.

Baked beans:

Ingredients: 2 large cans baked beans, ½ cup brown sugar; ¼ cup ketchup; ¼ cup BBQ sauce; 2 Tbsp. cider vinegar; 2 tsp. ground mustard; 1 tsp. pepper; 3 or 4 strips of bacon.

Directions: Pour excess liquid off beans and remove any chunks of pork fat. In a large bowl, mix all ingredients except bacon. Spray a rectangular pan with cooking oil and pour the bean mixture into it. Lay bacon across the top. Bake, uncovered at 300 degrees for about an hour.
Note: You can start the beans at 300 degrees and then increase the heat for the potatoes. Check for doneness after 45 minutes.

Oven Fries:

Ingredients: 6-8 potatoes, scrubbed and cut into sticks; seasoned salt; cooking oil spray.

Directions: Place cut potatoes in a large bowl. Sprinkle liberally with seasoning salt and spray with cooking oil spray. Toss to coat. Spray a large sided cookie sheet or jelly roll pan with cooking oil spray. Spread potatoes on the pan in a single layer. Bake at 375 degrees for 45 minutes, turning once.
*Note: you can add a couple tsp. chili powder when seasoning, if you want your fries to be spicier.

Day 3

Swiss chicken:

Ingredients: 6 boneless, skinless chicken breasts; 1 egg + 1 egg white; 1 sleeve Ritz crackers, crushed fine; 1 tsp. salt; ½ lb. fresh mushrooms, washed, stems removed, and sliced; 3 Tbsp. butter, divided; 6 slices ham; 6 slices Swiss cheese.

Directions: Place chicken breasts between 2 large sheets of plastic wrap or waxed paper. Pound breasts with a mallet (if you have one) or the bottom of a coffee cup (this is what I always do) until they are about ¼ inch thin. In a shallow bowl or pie plate, lightly beat the egg and the egg white; combine cracker crumbs and salt in another shallow bowl or pie plate. Dip chicken in egg, then in crumbs; set aside. (*Note: do all the dipping with one hand so you keep one clean. Or use tongs to dip chicken in egg mixture.) In a large oven-proof skillet, melt 1 Tbsp. butter and sauté mushrooms for about 3 minutes. Remove and set aside. Melt the remaining butter in the same skillet and add the chicken. Cook over medium heat for 4 minutes on each side or until juices run clear. Top each chicken breast with a ham slice, mushroom slices, and a Swiss cheese slice. Broil 4 inches from the heat for 1-2 minutes or until the cheese is melted.

Carrot and broccoli casserole:

Ingredients: 1 package baby carrots; 2 bunches fresh broccoli, cut into florets; 2 cans cheese soup; ¾ cup butter, divided; 1 sleeve Ritz crackers, crushed.

Directions: Place 1 inch of water in a saucepan; add carrots. Bring to a boil. Reduce heat and simmer 8 minutes. Add broccoli, cover and simmer another 8 minutes. Drain and set aside. In a small pan, cook and stir soup and ¼ cup butter until smooth. Pour soup mixture over drained vegetables and stir to coat. Transfer vegetables and soup mixture to a greased oblong casserole dish. Place crushed crackers in a bowl; melt the remaining butter and pour over crackers; stir to coat. Top vegetables with crumb mixture and bake uncovered at 350 degrees for 35-40 minutes.

Day 4

BBQ pork chops:

Ingredients: 6-8 boneless pork chops; Angie's spice rub; BBQ sauce.

Directions: Rub pork chops with spice rub. Grill 7-8 minutes on each side or until done. Brush with BBQ sauce during the last few minutes. Serve with extra sauce for dipping.

Twice- baked potato casserole:

Ingredients: 6 medium unpeeled potatoes, baked; ½ tsp. salt; ½ tsp. pepper; the remaining bacon from making the baked beans on Day 2, cooked and crumbled **OR** 1 jar fully cooked bacon bits; 3 cups (24 oz.) sour cream; 8 oz. mozzarella cheese, shredded; 8 oz. cheddar cheese, shredded; 2-4 green onions, chopped.

Directions: Bake potatoes for 1 hour at 350 degrees or until tender (you could do this part in the microwave). Cut baked potatoes into 1 inch cubes. Place half in a greased oblong casserole dish. Sprinkle with ½ the salt, paper, and bacon. Top with ½ the sour cream and cheeses. Repeat layers. Top with green onions. Bake at 350 for 20 minutes or until the cheese is melted.

Green beans:

Ingredients:2 cans green beans, ½ tsp. salt; ½ tsp. pepper; ½ tsp. thyme; 1 Tbsp. butter.

Directions: Melt butter in a saucepan. Add remaining ingredients; heat through.

Day 5

Layered ravioli casserole:

Ingredients: 2 packages frozen ravioli; 1 (15 oz.) can diced tomatoes; 1 (15 oz.) can tomato puree; 1 (15 oz.) can tomato sauce; 2 small cans Italian tomato paste; 1 Tbsp. basil; 1 Tbsp. parsley; 2 tsp. oregano; 3 cloves garlic, minced; 1 large onion, diced; 1 Tbsp. olive oil; 8 oz. mozzarella, shredded.

Directions: Heat oil in a large pot. Add onion and garlic and sauté until tender. Add all canned tomato products and herbs. Bring to a boil, reduce heat, and simmer 30 minutes. Grease a lasagna pan and spread about a cup of the sauce in it. Arrange 1 of the packages of frozen ravioli in the pan. Top with ½ the sauce and ½ the cheese. Repeat layers. Bake, covered, at 350 degrees for 45 to 60 minutes.

Caesar salad:

Ingredients: 3 Tbsp. olive oil; 4-1/2 tsp. lemon juice; 1 tsp. prepared mustard; 1 garlic clove, minced; 6-8 cups torn romaine lettuce (about 3 romaine hearts); cup croutons; ½ cup shredded Parmesan cheese.

Directions: In a jar with a tight-fitting lid, combine the oil, lemon juice, mustard, and garlic; shake well. In a large salad bowl, combine romaine, croutons, and cheese. Drizzle with Parmesan cheese and toss to coat.

Day 6

Sausage and egg casserole:

Ingredients: 1 lb. sausage, cooked and drained; ½ cup chopped green onions; 2 tomatoes, chopped; 8 oz. cheddar cheese, shredded; 1 cup Bisquick; 12 eggs; 1 cup milk; 1 tsp. salt; 1 tsp. pepper.

Directions: In a greased 3 qt. baking dish, layer the sausage, onions, tomatoes and cheese. In a large bowl, whisk the pancake mix, eggs, milk, salt and pepper. Pour over the cheese. Bake, uncovered, at 350 degrees for 45-50 minutes. Allow to stand for 10 minutes before serving.

Potato cakes:

Ingredients: 2 large potatoes, baked in the microwave and peeled; 2 large potatoes, peeled and grated; 2 cups flour; 1 tsp. baking soda; 1

½ cups buttermilk; 3+ Tbsp. butter or oil for frying; 1 tsp. salt; 1 tsp. pepper.

Directions: In a large mixing bowl, mash the baked potatoes with a fork. Stir in raw potatoes, flour, baking soda, salt, and pepper. Mix well with 1 cup buttermilk adding more as needed to make a stiff batter. Shape into patties. Melt butter in a large skillet. Fry potato cakes in butter until crispy and golden on both sides. You may need to add more butter to the pan as you continue making all the potato cakes.

Day 7

Beef stew (crock pot recipe):

Ingredients: 3-4 pounds stew meat or a roast that has been cut into bite-sized pieces; 2 Tbsp. oil; 1 cup flour; 1 tsp. salt; 1 tsp. pepper; 2 onions, chopped; 1 can diced tomatoes; 1 can beef broth; 1 garlic clove, minced; 1 Tbsp. parsley flakes; 1 bay leaf; 1 cup carrot slices; ½ cup celery slices; ½ cup frozen peas; 3-4 potatoes, peeled and cut into 2 inch pieces.

Directions: Heat oil in a large frying pan. Mix flour, salt, and pepper in a large mixing bowl. Place meat in flour, a little at a time, stirring around to coat. Brown the meat in oil, a little at a time, until all has been browned. Place meat and all remaining ingredients in a crock pot and cook on low 10-12 hours.
*Note: You can assemble this the night before and just plug and go in the morning.

Cheese scones:

Ingredients: 2 cups flour; 2 Tbsp. sugar; 1 Tbsp. baking powder; 1 tsp. salt; ¼ tsp. baking soda; 6 oz. cheddar cheese, shredded; 1 egg; ½ cup sour cream; ¼ cup oil; 3 Tbsp. milk.

Directions: In a large bowl, combine flour, sugar, baking powder, baking soda, salt, and cheese. In another bowl, combine egg, sour cream, oil, and milk; stir into dry ingredients just until moistened. Turn onto a floured surface and knead gently 10-12 times. Gently pat out into a ⅓ inch thickness. Cut with a biscuit cutter or cut into triangles with a knife. Place on a greases baking sheet and bake at 425 degrees for 15-20 minutes or until golden brown.

Appendix

I have included in this section a few of my canning recipes, my spice rub for meat, appetizers, and a few of my favorite desserts.

Canning Recipes

Hot Pepper Jelly (don't be afraid to try it!)

Ingredients: 25 jalapeño peppers; 2 yellow bell peppers; 2 green bell peppers; 2 red bell peppers; 4 ½ cups cider vinegar; 2 Tbsp. crushed red pepper flakes (optional); 19 ½ cups sugar; 3 pouches Certo liquid fruit pectin.

Directions: Wear rubber gloves when handling hot peppers (this is extremely important!). Cut the tops off each jalapeño pepper and cut in half lengthwise. Take your finger and run it down the center of the split pepper, removing the seeds. You should remove the seeds from about half of them. In a food processor, puree jalapeños and place in a large pot. Cut tops off of the bell peppers, remove seeds and puree in a food processor; add to the jalapeños. Pour vinegar and sugar into the pot. Bring to a boil. Stir in pepper flakes (if desired) and pectin. Return to a boil. Remove from heat. Ladle hot jelly into hot pint jars, leaving ¼ inch headspace. Adjust 2 piece caps. Process jars in a boiling water bath for 10 minutes. Remove and allow to cool on the counter top. Makes 11 pints.
*Note: Try this awesome snack (beware—very addicting!) top a wheat cracker with cream cheese and about a tsp. of the pepper jelly.

Sweet Heat Taco Sauce

Ingredients: 1 (6 lb. 15 oz.) can tomato paste (you can get this at bulk food stores); 14 cups water; 3 cups cider vinegar; 4 cups light corn syrup; 6 Tbsp. chili powder; 2 tsp. whole cumin seeds; 3 Tbsp. salt; 1 tsp. garlic salt; 1 garlic clove; 3 tsp. cayenne pepper; 3 tsp. hot pepper sauce (or more); 1 onion; 1 Fresno pepper; 4 jalapeño peppers; 1 chili pepper.

Directions: Puree onion, peppers, and garlic in a food processor. Combine all ingredients in a large pot. Bring to a boil. Reduce heat and simmer 1 hour, stirring occasionally. Ladle hot sauce into hot pint jars, leaving ¼ inch headspace. Adjust 2 piece caps. Process 30 minutes in a boiling water bath. Remove and allow to cool on the counter top. Makes 14 pints.

Italian Sauce

Ingredients: 1 Tbsp. oil; 2 large onions; 1 bulb garlic (not 1 clove— the whole thing!); 3 (15 oz.) cans tomato sauce; 1 (28 oz.) tomato sauce; 1 (6 lb. 15 oz.) can tomato paste; 8 cups water; ¼ cup basil; 2 Tbsp. oregano; 2 Tbsp. parsley; 1 Tbsp. thyme; 1 Tbsp. sugar; 1 Tbsp. salt; 1 Tbsp. pepper; 2 tsp. red pepper flakes (optional); 14 Tbsp. lemon juice, divided.

Directions: Heat oil in a large pot. Meanwhile, puree onions and garlic in a food processor. Add to the oil and sauté 2-3 minutes. Add remaining ingredients except lemon juice. Bring to a boil and reduce heat. Simmer 30 minutes. In each hot quart jar, place 2 Tbsp. lemon juice. Ladle hot sauce into hot jars, leaving ¼ inch headspace. Adjust 2 piece caps. Process 40 minutes in a boiling water canner. Remove and allow to cool on the counter top. Makes 7 quarts.

Salsa

Ingredients: 17 cups fresh tomatoes, peeled, cored, seeded, and chopped; 4 cups jalapeños, seeds removed from ½ and chopped; 3 large onions, chopped; 2 cups sweet peppers, chopped; 1 green bell pepper, chopped; 1 yellow bell pepper, chopped; 1 red bell pepper, chopped; 6 cloves garlic, minced; 2 Tbsp. dried cilantro (or ¼ cup fresh); 4 tsp. salt; 2 ½ cups cider vinegar; 4 Tbsp. lime juice; 3-4 Tbsp. chili powder; 2 tsp. cayenne; 2 tsp. whole cumin seeds; 6 oz. tomato paste.

Directions: Place all ingredients into a large pot and bring to a boil. Reduce heat and simmer ½ hour or until thickened. Ladle hot salsa into hot quart jars (approximately 12). Process in a boiling water canner for 30 minutes. Remove and allow to cool on the counter top. Makes 12 about quarts.

Dry Mixes

Hot Cocoa Mix

Ingredients: 2 ½ cups nonfat dry milk; 1 ½ cups powdered sugar; 3 cups Nesquick (or other dry chocolate milk mix); 1 ½ cups powdered nondairy creamer; ½ tsp. salt.

Directions: In a large mixing bowl, combine all ingredients and stir until well-mixed. Place cocoa mix in pint or quart sized canning jars. To serve, place about 2 Tbsp. mix in a coffee mug and fill with boiling water. Stir and allow to cool for a few minutes before drinking.

Angie's Spice Rub:

Ingredients: 1 Tbsp. black pepper; 2 Tbsp. ground cumin; 2 Tbsp. chili powder; 2 Tbsp. brown sugar; 1 Tbsp. white sugar; 1 Tbsp. dried basil; 4 Tbsp. paprika; 2 Tbsp. salt; 3 Tbsp. garlic powder; 1 Tbsp. Montreal steak seasoning; 2 Tsp. cayenne pepper.

Directions: In a large mixing bowl, combine all ingredients and stir until well-mixed. Store in a glass quart jar.

Appetizers

Peggy's Cheese Ball

Ingredients: 2 (8 oz.) bars cream cheese, softened; 3 tsp. Accent; 1 tsp. Worcestershire sauce; 1 tsp. garlic powder; 2 (3 oz.) packages dried beef, chopped fine; 8-10 green onions, chopped fine.

Directions: Place all ingredients in a mixing bowl. Mix it up with your hands or with a hand mixer. Form into a ball. Chill. Remove from refrigerator 20 minutes before serving. Serve with assorted crackers.

Pepper Jelly Cheese Ball

Ingredients: 2 (8oz.) bars cream cheese, softened; ¼ cup hot pepper jelly; 1 cup finely shredded cheddar cheese.

Directions: In a mixing bowl, combine cream cheese, pepper jelly, and ¼ cup cheddar cheese. Mix it up with your hands or a hand mixer. Shape into a ball. Place the remaining cheese on a sheet of waxed paper and roll cheese ball in the cheese to cover. Serve with wheat crackers.

Carmel Pecan Cheese Ball

Ingredients: 2 (8 oz.) bars cream cheese, softened; 14 caramels; 1 Tbsp. water; 1 cup pecans, chopped very fine.

Directions: To melt caramels, unwrap and place in a microwave safe container. Add 1 Tbsp. water and microwave for 30 seconds and stir until smooth. In a mixing bowl, combine cream cheese, caramel, and ½ cup pecans. Mix it up with your hands or a hand mixer. Shape into a ball. Place the remaining pecans on a sheet of waxed paper and roll cheese ball in the pecans to cover. Serve with cinnamon graham crackers.

Tortilla Roll-ups

Ingredients: 2 (8 oz.) bars cream cheese, softened; 1 package burrito-sized flour tortillas; 1 tsp. chili powder; 1 Tbsp. chopped jalapeños (I use the kind from the jar for this); salsa.

Directions: In a large mixing bowl, combine cream cheese, chili powder, and jalapeños. Mix with a hand mixer. Spread about a Tbsp. or so on each tortilla. Roll each tortilla up, pressing down after each roll. Slice the rolls into 1 ½ inch pieces. Serve with salsa.

Desserts:

Sandy's Chocolate Brownies:

Ingredients: Brownie ingredients: 2 sticks butter (melted); 2 cups sugar; 4 eggs; 2 tsp. vanilla extract; ½ cup cocoa powder; 1 ½ cups flour; 1 tsp. salt; cooking oil spray.
Icing ingredients: ½ stick butter, melted; 2 Tbsp. cocoa powder; 3 Tbsp. milk; 2-3 cups powdered sugar (sifted).

Directions: In a mixing bowl, combine 1 cup melted butter, sugar, eggs, 2 tsp. vanilla. Beat with a hand mixer. Add ½ cup cocoa powder, mix in with a spoon. Add flour and salt, mix with a spoon. Spray a jelly roll pan with cooking oil spray. Bake at 350 degrees for 15 minutes. While the brownies are cooling, make the icing. Melt ½ stick butter. Add cocoa powder and milk; stir until smooth. Add powdered sugar, a little at a time, until icing reaches a creamy consistency. Pour over brownies and spread.

Sandy's Butterscotch Brownies:

Ingredients: 1 cup butter; 4 cups brown sugar; 4 tsp. vanilla extract; 4 eggs; 3 cups flour; 4 tsp. baking powder; 2 tsp. salt; cooking oil spray.

Directions: In a small saucepan, melt butter. Remove from the heat. In a large mixing bowl, combine melted butter, vanilla, eggs, and sugar. Stir in remaining ingredients. Spray a jelly roll pan with cooking oil spray and spread batter in the pan. Bake for 20-25 minutes at 350 degrees. Cut into squares while warm.

145

Peanut Butter Cheesecake

Ingredients: Crust: 1 ½ cups crushed pretzels; ⅓ cup butter, melted. Filling: 5 (8oz.) packages cream cheese, softened; 1 ½ cups sugar; ¾ cup creamy peanut butter; 2 tsp. vanilla extract; 3 eggs; 1 cup peanut butter chips; 1 cup semi-sweet chocolate chips. Topping: 1 cup sour cream; 3 Tbsp. creamy peanut butter; ½ cup sugar; ½ finely chopped peanuts.

Directions: In a small bowl, combine pretzels and butter. Press onto the bottom and 1 inch up the sides of a greased 10 inch spring form pan. Place the pan on a cookie sheet and bake at 350 degrees for 5 minutes. Cool on a wire rack. In a mixing bowl, beat cream cheese and sugar until smooth. Add peanut butter and vanilla; mix well. Add eggs; beat on low until just combined. Stir in chips. Pour over the crust. Bake at 350 degrees for 50-55 minutes or until center is almost set. Cool on a wire rack for 15 minutes (leave the oven on). Meanwhile, in a mixing bowl, combine sour cream, peanut butter, and sugar; spread over filling. Sprinkle with nuts. Return to the oven for 5 minutes. Cool on a wire rack for 10 minutes. Carefully run a knife along the edge of the pan to loosen; cool one hour longer. Refrigerate overnight. Remove sides of pan and place on a serving plate before serving.

My Mom's Pecan Pie

Ingredients: 3 eggs, ⅓ cup sugar, dash salt, 1 cup dark corn syrup; cup melted butter; 2 cup pecan halves. Pie crust for 2 pies (recipe follows).

Directions: Place foil over the edges of the crusts. Beat eggs, add sugar and salt until dissolved. Stir in syrup and butter. Stir in pecans. Pour into crusts. Bake at 350 degrees for 25 minutes. Remove foil and bake 25 minutes longer.

Pie crust:

Ingredients: 4 cups flour; 1 ¾ cups shortening; 1 tablespoon sugar; 2 teaspoons salt; 1 tablespoon apple cider vinegar; 1 egg; ½ cup water

Directions: Mix flour, shortening, sugar, and salt together. In a small bowl, mix vinegar, egg and water. Beat well. Add this to the flour mixture. Blend until mixed. Shape into a ball and chill 15 minutes. Divide in half. Roll into a circle between parchment paper or wax paper. Roll it out until it's several inches larger than the pie pan. This makes two nine-inch single pie shells or one double.

Printed in the United Kingdom
by Lightning Source UK Ltd.
107257UKS00001B/43